ELECTRICITY AND MAGNETISM

STUDENT PHYSICS SERIES

General Editor:
Professor R.J. Blin-Stoyle, FRS
School of Mathematical and Physical Sciences
University of Sussex

Advisory Editors:
Professor E.R. Dobbs
University of London

Dr J. Goddard
City of London Polytechnic

ELECTRICITY AND MAGNETISM

Roland Dobbs

Hildred Carlile Professor of Physics
University of London

ROUTLEDGE & KEGAN PAUL
London, Boston, Melbourne and Henley

First published in 1984
by Routledge & Kegan Paul plc
39 Store Street, London WC1E 7DD, England
9 Park Street, Boston, Mass. 02108, USA
464 St Kilda Road, Melbourne,
Victoria 3004, Australia and
Broadway House, Newtown Road,
Henley-on-Thames, Oxon RG9 1EN, England

Set in IBM Press Roman
by Hope Services, Abingdon,
and printed in Great Britain
by Cox & Wyman Ltd, Reading

Library of Congress Cataloging in Publication Data

Dobbs, Roland, 1924–

Electricity and magnetism.
(Student physics series)
Includes index.
1. Electromagnetism.   I. Title.   II. Series.
QC760.D63   1984   537   83-23112

British Library CIP data available

ISBN 0-7102-0157-5

Contents

Preface

Electromagnetism is basic to our understanding of the properties of matter and yet is often regarded as a difficult part of an undergraduate physics course. In this book answers are developed from first principles to such questions as: What is electricity? What is electromagnetism? Why are some materials magnetic and others non-magnetic? What *is* magnetism?

Physics answers these questions in two related ways. On the one hand the *classical* explanation is in terms of classical concepts: electric charge q, electric and magnetic fields (**E** and **B**) and electric currents. On the other hand the *microscopic* (or 'atomic') explanation is in terms of quantum concepts: electrons, nuclei, electron orbits in atoms, electron spin and photons. Microscopic explanations underlie classical ones, but do not deny them. The great triumphs of classical physics are mechanics, gravitation, thermodynamics, electromagnetism and relativity. Historically they began at the time of Newton (seventeenth century) and were completed by Maxwell (nineteenth century) and Einstein (early twentieth century). Microscopic explanations began with J.J. Thomson's discovery of the electron in 1897. For most physical phenomena it is best to seek a classical explanation first, especially phenomena at room temperature, or low energy, when quantum effects are small. Although this text is primarily concerned with classical explanations in a logical, self-consistent sequence, they are related to microscopic (quantum) explanations at each stage.

The beauty of electromagnetism is that it can be summarised in just four equations: Maxwell's equations, which relate **E** and **B** in space with fixed and moving charges. The electromagnetic field equations due to Maxwell can lead to complicated solutions involving vector calculus (grad, div, curl), but are greatly simplified when we deal with *statics* — that is variables that do not depend on the time (t), or are stationary variables. Maxwell's equations then simplify and separate into two independent pairs of equations.

1. The first pair describe the electrostatic field **E** for fixed charges and are known as *Gauss's law* and the *circulation law*. They summarise electrostatics.
2. The second pair describe the magnetostatic field **B** for steady currents (charges moving at constant speed) and are known as *Gauss's law* and *Ampère's law*. They summarise magnetostatics.

In electrostatics only the **E** field appears and $\partial E / \partial t = 0$; in magnetostatics only the **B** field appears and $\partial B / \partial t = 0$. So under these conditions, electricity and magnetism are classically distinct, separate phenomena. But if you charge a capacitor (q varying with time) or move a magnet (**B** at a point varying with time) then **E** and **B** are no longer independent and new terms in the equations due to *electromagnetism* appear, as first discovered by Faraday (*Faraday's law*) and Maxwell (*Maxwell's law*).

The development of the subject in this text is therefore first electrostatics, then magnetostatics, followed by electromagnetism and magnetism. The final chapter summarises electromagnetism in terms of Maxwell's equations. These equations are then the beginning of the sequel to this book, *Electromagnetism*.

SI units are used throughout and are summarised in Appendix 1, which also gives their defining formulae and their dimensions in the MKSA system. The physical constants used in the text are listed in Appendix 2 with their approximate values and units. Vector operators are introduced at appropriate points and are summarised for the usual coordinate systems in Appendix 3. Each chapter, except the first and last, has a set of exercises (Appendix 4) with answers (Appendix 5).

Acknowledgments

This book owes much to the many undergraduates who have participated in my tutorials and lectures on electromagnetism at the Universities of Cambridge, Lancaster and London during the last twenty years.

Of the numerous texts I have studied, none has been so illuminating as volume 2 of the *Feynman Lectures on Physics* (Feynman, R.P., Leighton, R.B. and Sands, M., *Feynman Lectures on Physics*, vol. 2, London, Addison-Wesley, 1964), but any errors and obscurities in this brief summary of electricity and magnetism are entirely my responsibility.

It is a pleasure to thank Mrs Sheila Pearson for her accurate typing of the manuscript and my colleagues for their helpful comments and criticisms. I am indebted to the University of London for permission to reproduce some problems (marked L) from B.Sc. course unit examinations taken at the end of their first year by students reading physics at Bedford College.

Chapter 1
Introduction

Although all electromagnetic phenomena can be studied in empty space, an important part of any introductory course on electricity and magnetism is a proper understanding of the nature of matter. We shall therefore discuss dielectric behaviour in the chapter on electrostatics, conduction in metal wires in that on magneto-statics, and magnetism in matter (whether para-, dia- or ferro-magnetism) in the chapter on magnetism. In this first chapter the nature of matter is summarised.

All matter is composed of elementary particles, some charged positively (protons), some charged negatively (electrons) and some without charge (neutrons). The forces between these particles are of three different sorts, — gravitational, electrical and nuclear — which differ enormously in their strength and range.

The *gravitational force* was made famous by Newton in his studies of the planets and expressed by him in 1665 in the inverse square law of force between two masses m_1 and m_2

$$F_G = \frac{G\,m_1 m_2}{r^2} \qquad [1.1]$$

where r is the distance between m_1 and m_2 and G is the gravitational constant. The *electrical force* will be familiar as the law Coulomb found in 1785 for the force between electrical charges. This is another inverse square law of force. If r is now the distance between the charges q_1 and q_2, and K is an electrical constant

$$F_E = \frac{K\,q_1 q_2}{r^2} \qquad [1.2]$$

The third type of force between the elementary particles that constitute matter is a comparatively recent discovery. In 1932 Chadwick found that the nuclei of atoms and molecules contained not only protons but new particles — neutrons — and so there had to be a third type of force, the *nuclear force*, that held these particles together in the nucleus.

This nuclear force, composed of both weak and strong interactions, is exceedingly short range, falling off as $r^{-2} \exp(-r/r_0)$, where r_0 is about 10^{-15} m. In contrast the gravitational and electrical forces are comparatively long range (Fig. 1.1). It is

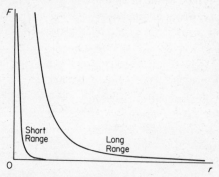

Fig. 1.1 Short-range and long-range forces.

obvious from the motion of the planets round the sun that gravitational forces are long range. It is not so obvious that electrical forces are similarly long range because electrical charges are usually screened by other charges of opposite sign at comparatively short range, so that the overall effect at long range is negligible.

Although both the gravitational and electrical force obey an inverse square law, their size differs enormously. For the proton–electron pair which comprises the hydrogen atom, the electrical force F_E is about 10^{39} or one thousand million million million million million million times as strong as the gravitational force F_G, as can be easily shown from equations [1.1] and [1.2] and a knowledge of the constants. So we can nearly always neglect gravitational effects in the presence of electrical forces. The exception is experiments like Millikan's oil drop, where the enormous mass of the earth acts on the oil drop with a force comparable to the electrical one exerted on the tiny charge of the oil drop as it moves between the charged plates.

The gravitational and electrical forces also differ in one other important respect: the gravitational force between particles of ordinary matter is always attractive, whereas the electrical force is repulsive (positive) between like charges and attractive (negative) between unlike charges. The net result is that large masses have large gravitational attractions for one another, but normally have negligible electrical forces between them.

The paradox is that although all matter is held together by electrical forces, of the interatomic or intermolecular or chemical-bond types, which are immensely strong forces, large objects are electrically neutral to a very high degree. The electrical balance between the number of protons and electrons is extraordinarily precise in all ordinary objects. To see how exact this balance is, Feynman has calculated that the repulsive force between two people standing at arm's length from each other who each had 1% more electrons than protons in their bodies would be enormous — enough in fact to repel a weight equal to that of the entire earth! So matter is electrically neutral because it has a perfect charge balance and this gives solids great stiffness and strength.

The study of electrical forces, electromagnetism, begins with Coulomb's law, equation [1.2]. All matter is held together by the electromagnetic interactions between atoms, between molecules and between cells, although the forces holding molecules and cells together are more complicated than the simple Coulomb interaction. The studies of condensed state physics, of chemistry and of biology are thus all dependent on an understanding of electromagnetism. This text develops the subject from Coulomb's law to Maxwell's equations, which summarise all the properties of the electromagnetic fields, in free space and matter. But if you ask why does the strong electrical attraction between a proton and an electron result in such comparatively large atoms rather than form a small electron–proton pair, you will not find the answer in Maxwell's equations alone. The study of electrical forces between particles at atomic or subatomic distances requires a new physics, quantum mechanics, which is the subject of the first book in the series.

Chapter 2
Electrostatics

Electric charge has been known since the Greeks first rubbed amber and noticed that it then attracted small objects. Little further progress was made until the eighteenth century when du Fay showed that there were two sorts of charge. One sort followed the rubbing of an amber rod with wool, the other a glass rod with silk. It was Benjamin Franklin who arbitrarily named the latter a positive charge and the original amber one a negative charge. He also showed that the total charge in a rubbing experiment was constant.

2.1 Coulomb's law

In 1785 Coulomb succeeded in discovering the fundamental law of electrostatics. A brilliant experimenter, he was able to invent and build a highly sensitive torsion balance with which he could measure precisely the relative force of repulsion between two light, insulating, pith balls when charged similarly and placed at different distances apart. He showed that this electrostatic force:
1. acts along the line joining the particles;
2. is proportional to the size of each charge; and
3. decreases inversely as the square of the distance apart.

It is therefore a long-range force (Fig. 1.1) and is given by the vector equation for the force $\mathbf{F}_1$ on charge q_1 due to charge q_2:

$$\mathbf{F}_1 = \frac{K q_1 q_2}{r_{12}^2} \hat{\mathbf{r}}_{12} \qquad [2.1]$$

where $\mathbf{r}_{12} = \mathbf{r}_1 - \mathbf{r}_2$, $r_{12}^2 = (x_1 - x_2)^2 + (y_1 - y_2)^2 + (z_1 - z_2)^2$

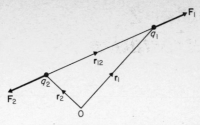

Fig. 2.1 Electrostatic forces between electric charges.

and $\hat{r}_{12}$ is a unit vector drawn *to 1 from 2* (Fig. 2.1) given by r_{12}/r_{12}. Fig. 2.1 shows that Newton's laws must apply and the force F_2 on charge q_2 due to q_1 is $F_2 = -F_1$. When both charges have the same sign, the force acts positively, that is the charges are repelled, while between a negative and a positive charge the force acts negatively and the charges are attracted.

For historical reasons the constant of proportionality K in equation [2.1] is not one, but is defined as:

$$K = \frac{1}{4\pi \epsilon_0} = 10^{-7}c^2 \qquad [2.2]$$

where ϵ_0 is the *electric constant* (permittivity of free space) and c is the velocity of light. The constant has to be determined from experiment. A recent value of $c = 2.997\,925 \times 10^8\,\mathrm{m\,s^{-1}}$ is accurate to better than 1 in 10^6, but for use in problems can be taken as $3.0 \times 10^8\,\mathrm{m\,s^{-1}}$. On the same basis $K = 9 \times 10^9\,\mathrm{N\,m^2\,C^{-2}}$, using the SI unit coulomb (C) for electric charge.

It is important to note that we have written in equation [2.1] Coulomb's law for charges in a *vacuum*; we have not mentioned the effects of a dielectric or other medium.

Principle of superposition

The only other basic law in electrostatics is the principle of superposition of electric forces. The principle states that if more than one force acts on a charge, then all the forces on that charge can be added vectorially into a single force. Thus for the total force on a charge q_1 due to charges q_2 at r_{12}, q_3 at r_{13}, etc., we have:

$$\mathbf{F}_1 = \mathbf{F}_{12} + \mathbf{F}_{13} + \ldots$$

$$\mathbf{F}_1 = K \left\{ \frac{q_1 q_2}{r_{12}^2} \, \hat{\mathbf{r}}_{12} + \frac{q_1 q_3}{r_{13}^2} \, \hat{\mathbf{r}}_{13} + \ldots \right\}$$

$$\mathbf{F}_1 = \frac{1}{4\pi\epsilon_0} \sum_j \frac{q_1 q_j}{r_{1j}^2} \, \hat{\mathbf{r}}_{1j}. \tag{2.3}$$

That the electric force between two small particles can be enormous is readily seen by estimating the force produced in Rutherford's scattering experiment when an alpha particle ($_2^4$He nucleus) makes a direct approach to a gold ($_{79}^{197}$Au) nucleus. The distance of closest approach is 2×10^{-14} m and so the maximum electrostatic repulsion is, from equations [2.1] and [2.2]:

$$F = \frac{2e \times 79e}{4\pi\epsilon_0 (2 \times 10^{-14})^2} = \frac{9 \times 10^9 \times 2 \times 79 e^2}{4 \times 10^{-28}} \text{ N.}$$

Since the charge on the proton, $e = 1.6 \times 10^{-19}$ C, the force on a single nucleus is about 100 newtons and a very strong force.

Electric field

The electric forces due to a distribution of electric charges, and particularly those due to a uniform distribution of charge, are best described in terms of an electric field vector, **E**, defined as the electric force per unit charge at a point. It can be visualised as the total force on a positive test charge, q at r_1, which is then allowed to become vanishingly small so as not to disturb the electric field. Using equation [2.3] we have:

$$\mathbf{E}(1) = \lim_{q \to 0} \frac{\mathbf{F}_1}{q} = \frac{1}{4\pi\epsilon_0} \sum_j \frac{q_j}{r_{1j}^2} \, \hat{\mathbf{r}}_{1j}. \tag{2.4}$$

This vector equation is a shorthand version of three much longer equations, which are nevertheless needed when a particular case has to be worked out.

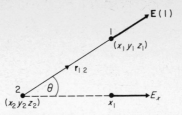

Fig. 2.2 The x-component E_x of electric field vector **E**.

For each coordinate plane there is a component of **E**(1) such as the x-component $E_x = E \cos\theta$ shown in Fig. 2.2. These components are therefore, for a charge q_2 at $(x_2 y_2 z_2)$

$$E_x(x_1 y_1 z_1) = \frac{q_2}{4\pi\epsilon_0} \frac{(x_1 - x_2)}{\{(x_1 - x_2)^2 + (y_1 - y_2)^2 + (z_1 - z_2)^2\}^{3/2}},$$

$$E_y(x_1 y_1 z_1) = \frac{q_2}{4\pi\epsilon_0} \frac{(y_1 - y_2)}{\{(x_1 - x_2)^2 + (y_1 - y_2)^2 + (z_1 - z_2)^2\}^{3/2}},$$

$$E_z(x_1 y_1 z_1) = \frac{q_2}{4\pi\epsilon_0} \frac{(z_1 - z_2)}{\{(x_1 - x_2)^2 + (y_1 - y_2)^2 + (z_1 - z_2)^2\}^{3/2}}.$$

Just writing out equation [2.4] in this way for Cartesian coordinates shows how useful vector equations are in saving time and space in print.

In a similar way we can write a vector equation for a charge distribution, using the notation shown in Fig. 2.3, where

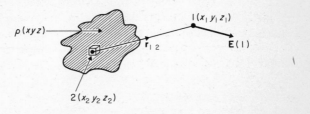

Fig. 2.3 The electric field **E**(1) at point 1 due to a distribution of charge.

$\rho(x, y, z)$ is the charge density, which produces a charge $\rho d\tau$ in a small volume $d\tau$. From equation [2.4] the electric field at point 1 is now:

$$E(1) = \frac{1}{4\pi\epsilon_0} \int_{\substack{\text{all} \\ \text{space}}} \frac{\rho(2) \, d\tau_2}{r_{12}^2} \hat{r}_{12} \qquad [2.5]$$

where r_2 is the variable and the integral $\int d\tau$ stands for $\int\int\int dx \, dy \, dz$ in Cartesian coordinates and similar triple integrals for other co-ordinate systems. To apply this equation one must again evaluate each component, for example:

$$E_y(x_1 y_1 z_1)$$
$$= \frac{1}{4\pi\epsilon_0} \int_{\substack{\text{all} \\ \text{space}}} \frac{(y_1 - y_2) \rho(x_2 y_2 z_2) \, dx_2 \, dy_2 \, dz_2}{\{(x_1 - x_2)^2 + (y_1 - y_2)^2 + (z_1 - z_2)^2\}^{3/2}}.$$

The equations [2.4] and [2.5] show, in principle, how all electrostatic fields can be obtained. Until the charges move there is no more to electricity: it is just Coulomb's law and the principle of superposition. In practice there are some clever tricks to avoid such horrible calculations that are only fit for computers. Remember too that, whatever happens, electric charge is always conserved *in toto*, since it depends ultimately on the stability of the electrons and protons in the universe. (Recent theories of elementary particles and of cosmology imply that the proton is not absolutely stable, but has a half-life $\sim 10^{31}$ years.)

2.2 Gauss's law

Gauss's law is about electric flux. The idea of the flux of a vector field arises from the flow of a fluid. We need a measure of the field lines (lines of force) coming out of a surface. We know that if we tilt the surface it has a maximum 'flow' when it is normal to the field lines and minimum (zero) when it is parallel to them (Fig. 2.4). If we describe the size of the surface by dS and its orientation by its unit normal vector $\hat{n}$, then the flux of the vector $\mathbf{E}$ from the element dS is defined as $\mathbf{E}.\hat{n}dS$. This is commonly abbreviated to $\mathbf{E}.\mathbf{dS}$, where $\mathbf{dS} = \hat{n}dS$ is a vector along the outward normal for outgoing flux. For a point charge q at the origin using equation [2.4] we have therefore:

$$\mathbf{E}.\mathbf{dS} = \frac{q}{4\pi\epsilon_0 r^2} \hat{r}.\mathbf{dS}. \qquad [2.6]$$

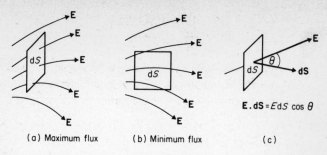

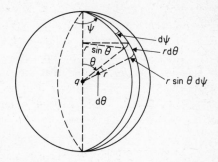

Fig. 2.4 Electric flux through various surfaces: (a) maximum for dS normal to **E**; (b) minimum for dS in plane of **E**; (c) flux of **E** is scalar product **E.dS**.

Fig. 2.5 Elementary surface area on a sphere around a point charge q.

The simplest way to evaluate this vector equation is to draw a sphere of radius r round the point charge and use spherical polar coordinates (r, θ, ψ), as in Fig. 2.5. The elementary area dS = $r \sin \theta \, \mathrm{d}\psi . r\mathrm{d}\theta$ and so the flux due to q through dS is:

$$\frac{q}{4\pi\epsilon_0 r^2} \, \hat{\mathbf{r}}.\mathbf{dS} = \frac{q}{4\pi\epsilon_0} \sin\theta \, \mathrm{d}\psi \mathrm{d}\theta$$

since $\hat{\mathbf{r}}$ and **dS** are parallel. Thus for an inverse square law of force, the flux from a point charge is independent of the distance r of the sphere from the point charge. The total flux through the sphere is:

$$\int_S \mathbf{E}.\mathbf{dS} = \int_S \frac{q}{4\pi\epsilon_0} \sin\theta \mathrm{d}\theta \mathrm{d}\psi$$

where the integral is taken over the surface S of the sphere. This is easily evaluated:

$$\int_S \mathbf{E} . \mathbf{dS} = \frac{q}{4\pi\epsilon_0} \int_0^\pi \sin\theta d\theta \int_0^{2\pi} d\psi = \frac{q}{\epsilon_0}. \qquad [2.7]$$

Of course a sphere is a particularly symmetrical surface to have chosen to find the total electric flux. Does it have to be so symmetrical to get such a simple answer? To find out we must evaluate equation [2.6] for a surface of arbitrary shape (Fig. 2.7) and this is best done by using the concept of a solid angle $d\Omega$ (Fig. 2.6). For any surface area dS whose normal $\mathbf{dS}$ makes an

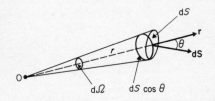

Fig. 2.6 Solid angle $d\Omega$ for cone of base dS.

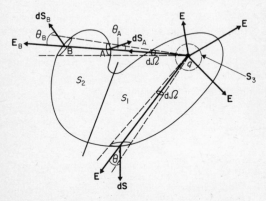

Fig. 2.7 Arbitrary surface around a point charge q.

angle θ with the radius vector $\mathbf{r}$ from an arbitrary point O, the solid angle $d\Omega$ is $d\Omega = dS \cos\theta/r^2$. We can therefore write equation [2.6] as

$$\mathbf{E}.\mathbf{dS} = q \, d\Omega/4\pi\epsilon_0$$

and use this expression for the electric flux through $\mathbf{dS}$ to evaluate the total flux through the arbitrary surface S.

We first divide S into two parts: S_1 that does enclose q; and S_2 that doesn't. Then for S_1 we must compute the $\int_{S_1} d\Omega$. Since q is a point charge, any surface S_1 that completely encloses q will subtend the same solid angle at q as the sphere S_3. Therefore:

$$\text{The flux through } S_1 = \frac{q}{4\pi\epsilon_0} \int_{S_3} d\Omega = \frac{q}{\epsilon_0}.$$

For the surface S_2 that does not enclose q, any flux cone must cut the surface twice, once on entry (e.g. at A) and once on exit (e.g. at B). The total flux flowing *out* of the surface bounded by A, B and the cone in between is therefore $\mathbf{E_B}.\mathbf{dS_B} - \mathbf{E_A}.\mathbf{dS_A}$. But

$$\frac{E_B}{E_A} = \frac{r_A{}^2}{r_B{}^2}$$

by the inverse square law for electric fields and

$$\frac{dS_B \cos\theta_B}{dS_A \cos\theta_A} = \frac{r_B{}^2 \, d\Omega}{r_A{}^2 \, d\Omega}$$

by definition of solid angles. The flux $\mathbf{E_A}.\mathbf{dS_A}$ that flows into this region is thus exactly the same as the flux $\mathbf{E_B}.\mathbf{dS_B}$ that flows out of the region and the net flux for the surface S_2:

$$\int_{S_2} \mathbf{E}.\mathbf{dS} = 0.$$

It follows, then, that the total flux for *any* surface surrounding q is

$$\int_S \mathbf{E}.\mathbf{dS} = \frac{q}{\epsilon_0} \qquad [2.8]$$

exactly as obtained from the sphere in equation [2.7].

By the principle of superposition the flux due to two charges q_1 and q_2 is just:

$$\int_S \mathbf{E_1}.\mathbf{dS} + \int_S \mathbf{E_2}.\mathbf{dS} = \frac{1}{\epsilon_0}(q_1 + q_2)$$

and it follows that the flux due to any charge distribution is:

$$\int_S \mathbf{E} \cdot \mathbf{dS} = \frac{1}{\epsilon_0} \int_V \rho d\tau. \qquad [2.9]$$

where V is the volume enclosed by S.

This is *Gauss's law:* the total flux out of any closed surface is equal to the total charge enclosed by it divided by the electric constant, ϵ_0.

Applications of Gauss's Law

Gauss's law is particularly useful for finding the electric field due to a symmetrical distribution of charge. In each case the Gaussian surface is chosen to suit the symmetry of the problem, as will be seen from three examples.

1. **E** *for a sphere of charge*

Suppose we have a sphere of uniform charge density ρ_0, then

$$Q = \int_\tau \rho d\tau = \frac{4}{3}\pi a^3 \rho_0,$$

as illustrated in Fig. 2.8, is its total charge.

We first draw an imaginary Gaussian surface S of radius R through the point P, where we wish to find **E**. Since the charge is uniformly distributed throughout Q, by symmetry **E** is everywhere radial from Q.

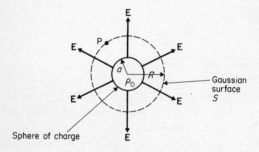

Fig. 2.8 Electric field of a sphere of charge.

Applying Gauss's law we obtain:

$$\int_S \mathbf{E}.\mathbf{dS} = \frac{Q}{\epsilon_0}.$$

Hence $\quad E.4\pi R^2 = Q/\epsilon_0$

or $\qquad\qquad E = Q/4\pi\epsilon_0 R^2.$

This is exactly the same as the field due to a point charge Q at the centre of the sphere of charge, a result that is quite hard to prove without Gauss's law.

2. **E** *for a line charge*

To find the electric field at a point distance r from an infinite line charge λ C m^{-1}, we note the cylindrical symmetry of the problem and draw a Gaussian cylindrical surface S (Fig. 2.9)

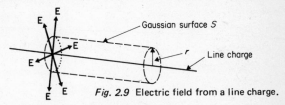

Fig. 2.9 Electric field from a line charge.

of radius r and of length 1 m. The electric vectors will be everywhere radial by symmetry and the same at all points along the line. Applying Gauss's law:

$$\int_S \mathbf{E}.\mathbf{dS} = \int_{\substack{\text{cylindrical} \\ \text{surface}}} \mathbf{E}.\mathbf{dS} + \int_{\substack{\text{end} \\ \text{faces}}} \mathbf{E}.\mathbf{dS} = \frac{\lambda}{\epsilon_0}.$$

Hence $\quad 2\pi r E + 0 = \lambda/\epsilon_0$

or $\qquad\qquad E = \lambda/2\pi\epsilon_0 r.$

3. **E** *for a plane sheet of charge*

To find the electric field near a plane sheet of charge σ C m^{-2}, we first note that **E** must be everywhere normal to the sheet and that the field $\mathbf{E}_1$ on one side must be the same size as the field $\mathbf{E}_2$ on the other side (Fig. 2.10). By symmetry our Gaussian surface S is a rectangular box whose sides parallel to the sheet of area A contain all the flux that the charges are producing. By Gauss's law:

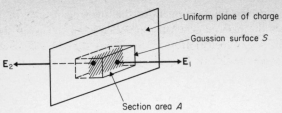

Fig. 2.10 Electric field from a sheet of charge.

$$\int_S \mathbf{E}.\,d\mathbf{S} = \int_A \mathbf{E}_1.\,d\mathbf{S} + \int_A \mathbf{E}_2.\,d\mathbf{S} = \frac{\sigma A}{\epsilon_0}.$$

Here both these integrals refer to outward fluxes, so:

$$EA + EA = \sigma A/\epsilon_0$$

or

$$E = \sigma/2\epsilon_0.$$

2.3 Electric potential

The electrostatic field, like the gravitational field, is a conservative field. The concept of potential energy used in gravitational problems can therefore be applied to electrical problems. In mechanics the work done, dW, on a particle travelling a distance ds along a path ab by an applied force $\mathbf{F}$ (Fig. 2.11) is given by the component of $\mathbf{F}$ acting in the direction s times ds,

$$dW = F \cos \theta \, ds.$$

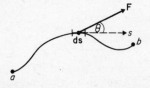

Fig. 2.11 Force $\mathbf{F}$ acting on a particle as it moves along the path ab.

The total work done over the path ab is then

$$W = \int_a^b (F \cos \theta) \, ds = \int_a^b \mathbf{F}.\,d\mathbf{S}$$

where **ds** is a vector element of the line from a to b. In electrostatics the particle becomes a test charge moving quasi-statically (with zero velocity) from a to b and the applied force must overcome the electric forces acting on the test charge. In Fig. 2.12

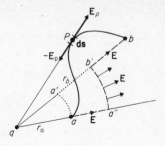

Fig. 2.12 Electric force $\mathbf{E}_p$ and external force $-\mathbf{E}_p$ acting on test charge at P, used in calculating the work done on taking unit charge from a to b.

the electric force on the test charge at P is $\mathbf{E}_p$ and so the external, applied force to move the charge quasi-statically is $-\mathbf{E}_p$. It is this force that is needed to calculate the external work done against the electric field due to the point charge q.

Therefore the work done on unit charge in taking it from a to b is

$$\int_a^b -\mathbf{E} \cdot \mathbf{ds}.$$

Using the definition of **E** in equation [2.4] and noting that $\hat{\mathbf{r}} \cdot \mathbf{ds} = \mathrm{d}r$, this integral becomes:

$$\frac{-q}{4\pi\epsilon_0} \int_a^b \frac{1}{r^2}\,\mathrm{d}r = \frac{-q}{4\pi\epsilon_0}\left(\frac{1}{r_a} - \frac{1}{r_b}\right).$$

Referring to Fig. 2.12 we can see that this amount of work would also be done if the charge was just moved radially from a' to b. Equally it would be the same if it was moved first along the radial path aa'', then along the circular path $a''b'$ and finally along the radial path $b'b$, since **E** is always normal to a circular path about q and therefore no work is done along a circular path.

It thus follows that the $\int_a^b \mathbf{E} \cdot \mathbf{ds}$ is the same along any arbitrary path which can always be considered as the zero sum of normal components along circular paths and the work done by the tangential components along radial paths. If the path is a closed loop C (a to b and back to a) then clearly the integral is zero:

$$\oint_C \mathbf{E} \cdot \mathbf{ds} = 0. \qquad [2.10]$$

This is the *circulation law* for the electrostatic field and is a characteristic of conservative fields that have spherical symmetry and of forces that are radial $f(\mathbf{r})$. It does not have to be an inverse square law force to have zero circulation.

When the path is not closed, the work done depends only on the end points and is independent of the path taken (Fig. 2.12). The work done on unit charge can therefore be represented as the difference between two electric potentials $\phi(b)$ and $\phi(a)$, by analogy with mechanical potential energy:

$$-\int_a^b \mathbf{E} \cdot \mathbf{ds} = \phi(b) - \phi(a). \qquad [2.11]$$

To obtain an absolute value for the electric potential, we must specify its zero. This is taken for convenience to be at an infinite distance from the source q so that

$$-\int_\infty^r \mathbf{E} \cdot \mathbf{ds} = \phi(r) \qquad [2.12]$$

defines the potential $\phi(r)$ at any point of distance r from q. Using equation [2.4] for $\mathbf{E}$, we obtain

$$\phi(r) = \frac{-q}{4\pi\epsilon_0}\left(\frac{1}{r}\right)$$

for a point charge q at the origin.

Electric potentials can be superimposed like electric fields and so for a distribution of charges we obtain similar equations to [2.4] and [2.5], namely:

$$\phi(1) = \frac{1}{4\pi\epsilon_0} \sum_i \frac{q_i}{r_{1i}} \qquad [2.13]$$

$$\text{and} \quad \phi(1) = \frac{1}{4\pi\epsilon_0} \int_{\substack{\text{all} \\ \text{space}}} \frac{\rho(2)\,d\tau_2}{r_{12}}. \qquad [2.14]$$

It is important to remember that electric potentials are the work done on unit charges and therefore measured in volts, not joules like potential energy. The volt is defined by: the work done is 1 joule when a charge of 1 coulomb is moved through a potential difference of 1 volt.

The calculation of electric fields can often be achieved more simply from electric potentials than from equations [2.4] and [2.5]. To do this we must invert equation [2.11] to obtain a differential equation. For two points distance Δx apart, by the definition of electric potential, the work done on moving charge through Δx is

$$\Delta W = \phi(x + \Delta x, y, z) - \phi(xyz)$$

$$= \frac{\partial \phi}{\partial x} \Delta x.$$

But the work done against the electric field **E** is

$$\Delta W = - \int_x^{x+\Delta x} \mathbf{E}.\mathbf{ds} = -E_x \Delta x.$$

Hence $E_x = -\dfrac{\partial \phi}{\partial x}$.

Similarly, for movements along Δy and Δz we find:

$$E_y = -\frac{\partial \phi}{\partial y} \quad \text{and} \quad E_z = -\frac{\partial \phi}{\partial z},$$

so that $\quad \mathbf{E} = -\left(\dfrac{\partial \phi}{\partial x} \mathbf{i} + \dfrac{\partial \phi}{\partial y} \mathbf{j} + \dfrac{\partial \phi}{\partial z} \mathbf{k} \right) \qquad [2.15]$

where $(\mathbf{i}, \mathbf{j}, \mathbf{k})$ are unit vectors along the Cartesian axes $0x, 0y, 0z$.

In vector calculus the gradient of a scalar field $\Omega(xyz)$ that is continuously differentiable is defined as the vector

$$\text{grad } \Omega = \frac{\partial \Omega}{\partial x} \mathbf{i} + \frac{\partial \Omega}{\partial y} \mathbf{j} + \frac{\partial \Omega}{\partial z} \mathbf{k} \qquad [2.16]$$

Comparing equations [2.15] and [2.16] we see that the electrostatic field **E** is just minus the gradient of the electric potential ϕ:

$$\mathbf{E} = -\text{grad } \phi \qquad [2.17]$$

It follows that electric fields have the convenient unit of volts per metre, as well as the more fundamental one of newtons per coulomb from equation [2.4].

Conductors

A metal may be considered as a conductor containing many 'free' electrons which can move about inside but not easily escape from the surface. Inside a metal there is perfect charge balance between the positive ions and the negative electrons and, on a macroscopic scale, the net charge density is zero. By Gauss's law the electric field $\mathbf{E}_i$ inside a Gaussian surface that coincides with the surface of a metallic conductor (Fig. 2.13(a)) must therefore also be zero.

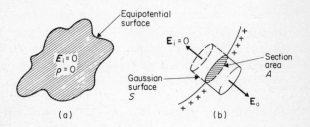

Fig. 2.13 (a) Electric field inside a conductor is zero. (b) Outside a charged conductor it depends on the charge density at the surface σ Cm^{-2}.

By equation [2.17] the gradient of the electric potential at the surface, grad ϕ, must be zero and so the surface of a conductor is an equipotential surface and the interior of the conductor is an equipotential region (ϕ = constant).

When a conductor is charged the excess charges stay on the surface, where they are not completely free. They then produce an external field $\mathbf{E}_0$ just outside the surface (Fig. 2.13(b)), whose value can be obtained from the cylindrical Gaussian surface S of cross-sectional area A and cylindrical axis normal to the surface. Clearly

$$\int_S \mathbf{E} \cdot \mathbf{dS} = E_0 A + 0 = \frac{\sigma A}{\epsilon_0}$$

and $E_0 = \sigma/\epsilon_0$. [2.18]

This is just *twice* the field for a sheet of charge (section 2.2) because the internal electrons have produced zero internal field when the 'sheet of charge' is no longer isolated, but on a conductor. A similar result is seen if we consider two uniformly charged, parallel, conducting plates. In Fig. 2.14 the large

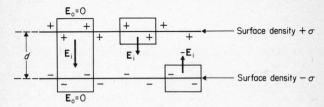

Fig. 2.14 Electric field between two charged plates.

Gaussian surface encloses a total charge of zero and so the external field $\mathbf{E}_0 = 0$. On the other hand the internal field $\mathbf{E}_i$, whether obtained from the positively charged plate, or the negatively charged plate, is just $E_i = \sigma/\epsilon_0$.

An interesting question is: can the inner surface of a hollow conductor be charged? In Fig. 2.15 if there is a surface density of charge σ inside the cavity then there is an electric field in the cavity and for the closed path C through P and Q:

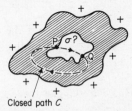

Fig. 2.15 Can the inner surface of a hollow conductor be charged?

$$\oint_C \mathbf{E}.\mathbf{ds} \neq 0.$$

But this would violate the circulation law (equation [2.10]) and so $\mathbf{E}$ inside a cavity must be zero and it is impossible to charge the inside of a hollow conductor. This important principle is the basis of electrostatic screening (the Faraday cage).

2.4 Electrostatic energy

Electric energy is stored in capacitors, for example in parallel plate capacitors (Fig. 2.14). From equation [2.11] we see that the potential difference V between the plates, for a uniform field $\mathbf{E}_i$ between the plates distance $\mathbf{d}$ apart is:

$$\mathbf{E}_i.\mathbf{d} = \phi_+ - \phi_- = V.$$

But $E_i = \sigma/\epsilon_0$ and for a uniform distribution of charge, $\sigma = Q/A$, where Q is the total charge on the plates of area A.

Hence $\quad V = \left(\dfrac{d}{\epsilon_0 A}\right) Q, \quad$ or $\quad V \propto Q.$

The proportionality between V and Q is always found for two oppositely charged conductors, since it arises from the principle of superposition: doubling the charges doubles the field and doubles the work done. By convention, we define *capacitance* by:

$$Q = CV$$

and so for the parallel plate capacitor the capacitance is

$$C = \epsilon_0 A/d. \tag{2.19}$$

The unit of capacitance is the farad (after Faraday) and is a coulomb per volt. It is a very large unit and typical small capacitors are in microfarad (μF) for use at low frequencies and in picofarad (pF) for radio frequencies. When capacitors are in parallel they are all at the same potential (Fig. 2.16(a)) and so $C = \sum\limits_i C_i$, but when they are in series they each carry the same charge (Fig. 2.16(b)) and then $1/C = \sum\limits_i 1/C_i$.

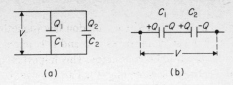

Fig. 2.16 Capacitors connected (a) in parallel and (b) in series.

The work done in charging a capacitor is equal to the *energy U* stored in it and so:

$$U = \int_0^Q V dQ = \frac{1}{C} \int_0^Q Q dQ = \frac{Q^2}{2C} = \frac{1}{2} CV^2. \qquad [2.20]$$

For the parallel plate capacitor, neglecting end-effects, the energy is:

$$U = \frac{Q^2}{2C} = \frac{(\sigma A)^2}{2(\epsilon_0 A/d)} = \frac{\sigma^2 A d}{2\epsilon_0}.$$

The *energy density u* in this electrostatic field is the total energy U divided by the volume Ad and so

$$u = \frac{\sigma^2}{2\epsilon_0} = \frac{1}{2} \epsilon_0 E^2 \qquad [2.21]$$

since $E = \sigma/\epsilon_0$ between the plates. This expression for the energy density was derived from a specific example, the parallel plate capacitor, but it contains only the electric field E and the electric constant ϵ_0. It is, in fact, quite general, as can be seen from Fig. 2.17. There an electric field is described by a number of equipotentials $\phi_1, \phi_2, \ldots$ and we can imagine any small volume $d\tau$ in that field as a tiny parallel plate capacitor ABCD, since a

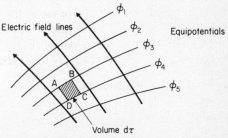

Fig. 2.17 Equipotentials in an electric field.

conducting plate is an equipotential surface. Therefore quite generally

$$U = \frac{1}{2} \epsilon_0 \int_\tau E^2 \, d\tau. \qquad [2.22]$$

The idea that the electrostatic energy is stored *in the electric field* is an important one and enables the energy to be computed without knowing anything about the distribution of electric charge. It is even more important in discussing the energy of radio waves. Clearly radio stations transmit electromagnetic energy in the waves we receive at our aerials, but they do not transmit electric charges over long distances. The energy is stored, and travels, in the electromagnetic field of the wave.

There is one point of difficulty in calculating electric fields. The energy of a charged sphere of radius a (problem 2) is $\frac{1}{2}Q^2/(4\pi\epsilon_0 a)$ and so the self-energy of a point charge $(a \rightarrow 0)$ would be infinite! Obviously the idea of stored energy in an electrostatic field is not consistent with the presence of point charges: either the electron has a finite size or we cannot extend our concept to elementary charged particles. To avoid this real difficulty we compute the energy only of the electrostatic fields between the charges, and omit their self-energy. Thus we can write equation [2.22] more generally as:

$$U = \frac{1}{2} \epsilon_0 \int_\tau \mathbf{E} . \mathbf{E} \, d\tau. \qquad [2.23]$$

Electric stress

The limit to the energy that can be stored in a particular capacitor depends on the maximum electric field E that its insulation will withstand before it breaks down under the electric stress. Typically the insulation strength is about $10^8 \, \text{V m}^{-1}$ so that a large capacitor of internal volume $0.1 \, \text{m}^3$ would hold a maximum of $\frac{1}{2}\epsilon_0 . 10^{16} . 0.1 \simeq 5 \, \text{kJ}$. This is small compared with the $10 \, \text{MJ}$ of chemical energy in $1 \, \text{kg}$ of common salt and very small compared with the $50 \, \text{TJ}$ of nuclear energy in $1 \, \text{kg}$ of uranium.

Still larger capacitors cannot easily be built because of the enormous mechanical stresses they are subjected to when charged.

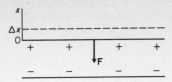

Fig. 2.18 Work is done in separating charged capacitor plates.

This can be seen by applying the principle of virtual work to charged capacitor plates (Fig. 2.18). If **F** is the attractive force between the plates, then the external work done ΔU increasing the separation by Δx must equal the change in electrostatic energy for constant Q. Using equations [2.19] and [2.20],

$$\Delta U = -F \Delta x = \tfrac{1}{2} Q^2 \Delta \left(\frac{1}{C}\right) = \frac{Q^2 \Delta x}{2\epsilon_0 A}$$

or $F = -Q^2/2\,\epsilon_0 A.$

But the charge $Q = \sigma A$ and the electric field is $E = \sigma/\epsilon_0$, so that the stress is:

$$\frac{F}{A} = \frac{1}{2}\,\epsilon_0 E^2.$$

This is the same as the energy density (equation [2.21]) and so for $E = 10^8\,\mathrm{Vm^{-1}}$, the mechanical stress is $\simeq 50\,\mathrm{kN\,m^{-2}}$ or about 5 tonne weight per square metre.

2.5 Dielectrics

Dielectric materials — like glass, paper and plastics — are electrical insulators. They have no free charges and do not conduct electricity, but they do influence electric fields. Faraday discovered that inserting an insulator between the plates of a parallel plate capacitor increased its capacitance. We define the *dielectric constant* (or relative permittivity) ϵ_r of an insulator from Faraday's experiment as the ratio of the capacitances when the capacitor is completely filled by the insulator to when it is empty:

$$\epsilon_r = C_{\text{full}}/C_{\text{empty}}. \qquad [2.24]$$

For commercial dielectrics the material is normally of uniform composition and when used in low electric fields is a linear, isotropic, homogeneous medium characterised by a single constant ϵ_r. Typical values of ϵ_r are air = 1.0006, polythene = 2.3, glass = 6, barium titanate ceramic = 3000. In designing capacitors, transformers, coaxial cables, etc., ϵ_r is an important factor influencing the design.

Physically there is a great deal to investigate in the dielectric behaviour of gases, liquids and, especially, solids, where ϵ_r can be an anisotropic parameter described by an appropriate tensor. The dielectric 'constant' will also vary with temperature, with the frequency of an electromagnetic field and will become nonlinear in high electric fields. It is only in its familiar usage in low-frequency, low-field capacitors that it can be treated as a simple constant.

Polarisation

What happens when a slab of dielectric is inserted into a parallel plate capacitor (Fig. 2.19)? We know that the capacitance

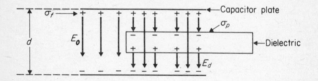

Fig. 2.19 Electric fields in a capacitor with and without a dielectric.

$C = Q/V$ increases from Faraday's experiment and so, if the charge Q on the plates has not leaked away, the potential V must have been reduced. Ignoring end-effects there is a uniform electric field $E = V/d$, so the electric field in the presence of the dielectric E_d must be less than that originally present, E_0. We can explain this by postulating an induced surface charge σ_p on each side of the dielectric slab, providing the charges are of opposite sign to those inducing them from the respective capacitor plates. If these free charges have surface density σ_f, then

$$E_d = \frac{\sigma_f - \sigma_p}{\epsilon_0} < \frac{\sigma_f}{\epsilon_0} = E_0 \qquad [2.25]$$

using the expression $E = \sigma/\epsilon_0$, which depends only on Gauss's law. This process is called *polarisation* of the dielectric and occurs only in the presence of the electric field (the part of the dielectric outside the capacitor plates is not polarised – Fig. 2.19).

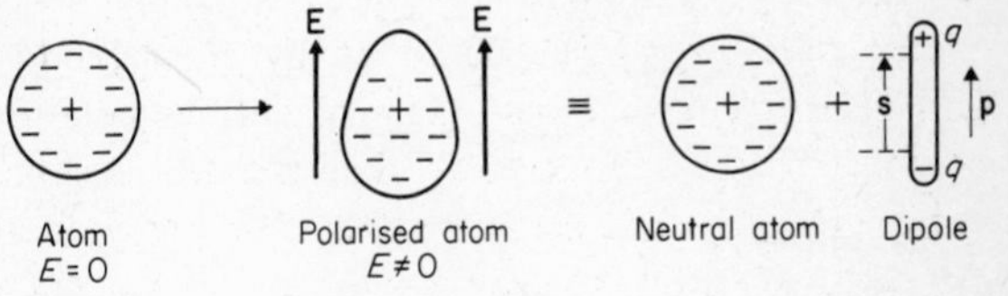

Fig. 2.20 Polarisation of an atom gives it a dipole moment **p**.

One way in which a neutral atom can acquire a dipole moment is shown in Fig. 2.20. The spherical electron cloud of the neutral atom is distorted by the applied electric field **E** and this distorted charge distribution is equivalent, by the principle of super-position, to the original spherical distribution plus a dipole distribution whose *dipole moment* is

$$\mathbf{p} = q\mathbf{s} \qquad [2.26]$$

where **s** is the distance vector from $-q$ to $+q$ of the dipole.

If a polarised dielectric consists of N such dipoles per unit volume, then we define its *polarisation* **P** as:

$$\mathbf{P} = N\mathbf{p} = \sum_i \mathbf{p}_i/\tau$$

where τ is the total volume. The SI unit of dipole moment is the coulomb-metre and that of polarisation coulomb per square metre. Going back to Fig. 2.19, we see that the surface charge on the dielectric is σ_p coulombs per square metre. If we assume this is due to N electrons per unit volume being displaced upwards a distance δ at each surface of area A', then the total charge is

$$\sigma_p A' = Ne\delta A'$$

or $\quad \sigma_p = Ne\delta.$

But $Ne\delta$ is just Np and so $P = \sigma_p$ and equation [2.25] becomes

$$E_d = \frac{\sigma_f - P}{\epsilon_0}.$$

From this equation it is clear that $\epsilon_0 E_d$ and P have the same dimensions. We define *electric susceptibility* χ_e, a dimensionless quantity, as the ratio:

$$\chi_e = P/\epsilon_0 E_d.$$

Knowing χ_e for our dielectric material we therefore obtain the reduced electric field E_d as

$$E_d = \frac{\sigma_f}{\epsilon_0} \left(\frac{1}{1 + \chi_e} \right). \qquad [2.27]$$

The capacitance of the capacitor is inversely proportional to the potential and so to the electric field. Using equations [2.24], [2.25] and [2.27] we therefore obtain

$$\epsilon_r = \frac{E_0}{E_d} = (1 + \chi_e). \qquad [2.28]$$

Measurement of the electric susceptibility χ_e of matter at low frequencies is thus a measurement of the dielectric constant ϵ_r, which at optical frequencies can be shown to be the square of the refractive index (see the sequel to this text, *Electromagnetism*).

Electric displacement

For all electrostatic systems we have the fundamental equation (equation [2.9]), Gauss's law:

$$\int_S \mathbf{E} \cdot \mathbf{dS} = \frac{1}{\epsilon_0} \int_V \rho \, d\tau$$

where V is the volume enclosed by the surface S.

When dielectrics are present, the charge density ρ will be the sum of any polarisation charges of density ρ_p and any free charges of density ρ_f. Therefore

$$\epsilon_0 \int_S \mathbf{E} . \mathbf{dS} = \int_V \rho_f \, d\tau + \int_V \rho_p \, d\tau. \qquad [2.29]$$

We have seen (Fig. 2.19) that in a parallel plate capacitor, when the polarisation $\mathbf{P}$ is normal to the surface of the dielectric, its magnitude is just the surface density of charge σ_p displaced from inside the dielectric. At the ends of the dielectric slab where $\mathbf{P}$ is tangential to the surface the surface density of charge is zero. It is the normal component of $\mathbf{P}$ that produces a surface charge, so that for an arbitrary surface S inside a dielectric (Fig. 2.21)

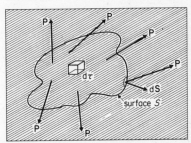

Fig. 2.21 Non-uniform polarisation of a dielectric.

the charge dq_p displaced across a surface element $\mathbf{dS}$ is $\mathbf{P} . \mathbf{dS}$. A non-uniform polarisation at the surface S therefore produces a total displacement of charge q_p across S given by:

$$q_p = \int_S \mathbf{P} . \mathbf{dS}$$

Since the dielectric is electrically neutral this is compensated by a volume density of charge $-\rho_p$ such that

$$\int_V - \rho_p \, d\tau = -q_p.$$

Hence the flux of $\mathbf{P}$ is given by a type of Gauss's law for polarised dielectrics:

$$\int_S \mathbf{P} . \mathbf{dS} = - \int_V \rho_p \, d\tau.$$

Combining this with equation [2.29], we have:

$$\int_S (\epsilon_0 \mathbf{E} + \mathbf{P}) . \mathbf{dS} = \int_V \rho_f \, d\tau$$

and define the *electric displacement*, $\mathbf{D}$, as

$$\mathbf{D} = \epsilon_0 \mathbf{E} + \mathbf{P} = \epsilon_0 (1 + \chi_e) \mathbf{E} \qquad [2.30]$$

so that Gauss's law can also be written:

$$\int_S \mathbf{D} \cdot d\mathbf{S} = \int_V \rho_f \, d\tau.$$ [2.31]

The flux of $\mathbf{D}$ thus depends solely on the free charges and this can be very useful, for example, in microwave physics.

However if we use this equation and, from [2.28] and [2.30], write

$$\mathbf{D} = \epsilon_r \, \epsilon_0 \, \mathbf{E}$$ [2.32]

then we must remember that for many materials ϵ_r is not just a number. As we have emphasised before, $\mathbf{P}$ (and hence $\mathbf{D}$) is not proportional to $\mathbf{E}$ for nonlinear materials and, in any case, χ_e (and so ϵ_r) can vary with frequency, temperature, crystal direction, etc. This is one reason why ϵ_r is often referred to as the relative permittivity rather than the dielectric constant of a dielectric.

Boundary conditions

What happens to the electric field when it crosses the boundary between two dielectrics of permittivities $\epsilon_1 = \epsilon_r(1)\epsilon_0$ and $\epsilon_2 = \epsilon_r(2)\epsilon_0$? To find out we apply Gauss's law as given in equation [2.31] and the circulation law, equation [2.10], to the electric vectors $\mathbf{D}$ and $\mathbf{E}$ shown in Fig. 2.22.

For the flux into and out of the Gaussian cylinder of cross-section dS and negligible height we have:

$$\mathbf{D}_1 \cdot d\mathbf{S}_1 + \mathbf{D}_2 \cdot d\mathbf{S}_2 = 0$$

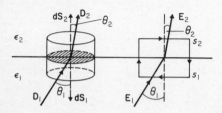

Fig. 2.22 Boundary conditions for the electric vectors $\mathbf{D}$ and $\mathbf{E}$ crossing between two dielectrics of permittivities ϵ_1 and ϵ_2.

since there are no free charges in dielectrics. Hence only the normal component D_n of each electric displacement contributes and

$$D_{1n} = D_{2n}. \qquad [2.33]$$

Applying the circulation law to the electric fields $\mathbf{E_1}$ and $\mathbf{E_2}$ crossing the closed loop of length $s_1 + s_2$, we have:

$$\oint_C \mathbf{E.ds} = \mathbf{E_1.s_1} + \mathbf{E_2.s_2} = 0.$$

Since we can contract the loop to be as near as we wish to the surface, only the tangential component E_t of each electric field contributes and

$$E_{1t} = E_{2t}. \qquad [2.34]$$

At the boundary we therefore have continuity for D_n and E_t. When it is valid to use equation [2.32] we can write [2.33] and [2.34] as:

$$\epsilon_{r1} E_1 \cos \theta_1 = \epsilon_{r2} E_2 \cos \theta_2$$

$$E_1 \sin \theta_1 = E_2 \sin \theta_2.$$

We therefore get refraction of $\mathbf{D}$ and $\mathbf{E}$ at the boundary with the relation

$$\frac{\tan \theta_1}{\tan \theta_2} = \frac{\epsilon_{r1}}{\epsilon_{r2}}. \qquad [2.35]$$

Energy density

For a vacuum parallel plate capacitor we showed that the energy stored in it is (equation [2.19]):

$$U = \frac{1}{2} CV^2.$$

With a dielectric completely filling it, the capacitance is increased by a factor ϵ_r (equation [2.24]) and the electric field is reduced by ϵ_r (equation [2.28]). Hence the energy stored is:

$$U = \frac{1}{2} \left(\frac{\epsilon_r \epsilon_0 A}{d} \right) (Ed)^2$$

where E is the reduced field. Therefore the energy density is:

$$u = \frac{1}{2} \epsilon_r \epsilon_0 E^2 = \frac{1}{2} DE,$$

where equation [2.32] applies. As with the energy density in the vacuum (Fig. 2.17), the energy density still resides in the electric field. The difference is that equation [2.23] now becomes in general:

$$U = \frac{1}{2} \int_\tau \mathbf{D} . \mathbf{E} \, d\tau. \qquad [2.36]$$

We can apply the principle of virtual work to the force between two capacitance plates (charged conductors) in a dielectric liquid (Fig. 2.18, with a dielectric present) and find

$$F = \frac{-\delta U}{\partial x} = \frac{-Q^2}{2} \frac{\partial}{\partial x} \left(\frac{1}{C} \right).$$

The dielectric increases C by a factor ϵ_r and so decreases F by $1/\epsilon_r$. However this only leads to a revised Coulomb's law (compare equation [2.3]) in certain cases:

$$\mathbf{F}_1 = \frac{1}{4\pi \epsilon_r \epsilon_0} \sum_j \frac{q_1 q_j}{r_{1j}^2} \hat{\mathbf{r}}_{1j}.$$

It is limited to dielectrics which are isotropic, homogeneous, linear and have a constant relative permittivity ϵ_r. In practice this limits it to fluids over a narrow range of temperature and pressure, whereas the vacuum version of Coulomb's law is always true for stationary charges.

Chapter 3
Electric potential and fields

The electrostatic field **E** is a vector field which, by equation [2.17], is just the gradient of a scalar field ϕ, the electric potential:

$$\mathbf{E} = -\text{grad } \phi.$$

The two most important properties of a vector field are its flux and its circulation. For the electrostatic field these are expressed by the integral equations [2.9] and [2.10]:

Gauss's law $$\int_S \mathbf{E}.\mathbf{dS} = \frac{1}{\epsilon_0} \int_V \rho \mathrm{d}\tau$$

Circulation law $$\oint_C \mathbf{E}.\mathbf{ds} = 0.$$

In this chapter theorems from vector analysis are used to derive the differential forms of these equations and hence to describe the electric potentials and fields for a number of cases of practical importance.

3.1 Poisson's and Laplace's equations

For an arbitrary vector field $\mathbf{F}(\mathbf{r})$ the flux out of a closed surface S enclosing a small volume $\mathrm{d}\tau$ is $\int_S \mathbf{F}.\mathbf{dS}$ where **dS** is the outward normal from $\mathrm{d}S$ (cf. Fig. 2.4). The flux of **F** per unit volume at the point **r** is called the *divergence* of **F** and is given by the limit of $\mathrm{d}\tau$ tending to zero:

$$\text{div } \mathbf{F} = \lim_{\mathrm{d}\tau \to 0} \frac{\int_S \mathbf{F}.\mathbf{dS}}{\mathrm{d}\tau}. \tag{3.1}$$

Gauss's divergence theorem follows from this definition and equates the total flux of a vector field **F** out of a closed surface S to the volume integral of the divergence of **F** over the volume V enclosed by S:

$$\int_S \mathbf{F}.\mathbf{dS} = \int_V \text{div } \mathbf{F} \, d\tau. \qquad [3.2]$$

The theorem applies to any vector field **F(r)** that is a smoothly varying field, that is **F(r)** is a continuously differentiable function of the coordinates of **r**.

Applying this theorem to Guass's law for the electrostatic field **E**, we have:

$$\int_S \mathbf{E}.\mathbf{dS} = \int_V \text{div } \mathbf{E} \, d\tau = \frac{1}{\epsilon_0} \int_V \rho d\tau$$

and so $\quad \text{div } \mathbf{E} = \rho/\epsilon_0 \qquad [3.3]$

where ρ is the total electric charge density and ϵ_0 is the electric constant. Alternatively, from equation [2.31] we can write:

$$\text{div } \mathbf{D} = \rho_f \qquad [3.4]$$

where ρ_f is the volume density of the free charges. The divergence of **E** or **D** will be zero when their outward and inward fluxes for a volume V are equal and opposite. This corresponds to the net charge density in the volume V being zero. Equations [3.3] and [3.4] show that the divergence of a vector field is a scalar field.

The circulation of a vector field **F(r)** around a closed loop C is $\oint_C \mathbf{F}.\mathbf{ds}$ and the circulation per unit area of the loop dS is used to define the *curl* of **F**. In general the circulation per unit area will depend on the orientation of dS relative to **F** and so the curl of **F** is a vector quantity, which is defined in terms of its component (curl **F**).$\hat{\mathbf{n}}$ normal to dS (Fig. 3.1), the direction of curl **F** being defined by a right-handed screw. Like the divergence, the curl of **F** is given by the limit of dS tending to zero:

$$(\text{curl } \mathbf{F}).\hat{\mathbf{n}} = \lim_{dS \to 0} \frac{\oint_C \mathbf{F}.\mathbf{ds}}{dS}. \qquad [3.5]$$

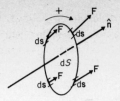

Fig. 3.1 Right-handed screw to evaluate curl **F**.

Stokes's theorem follows from this definition and equates the circulation of a vector field **F** around a closed loop C to the flux of curl **F** through any surface S bounded by C:

$$\oint_C \mathbf{F}.\mathbf{ds} = \int_S (\text{curl } \mathbf{F}).\mathbf{dS}. \qquad [3.6]$$

Applying this theorem to the circulation law for the electrostatic field **E**, we have the important result:

$$\text{curl } \mathbf{E} = 0. \qquad [3.7]$$

The fact that the electrostatic field is a curl-free field makes electrostatic problems the most straightforward ones to solve in electromagnetism.

In vector calculus the differential operator *del* is defined by:

$$\nabla = \mathbf{i}\frac{\partial}{\partial x} + \mathbf{j}\frac{\partial}{\partial y} + \mathbf{k}\frac{\partial}{\partial z} \qquad [3.8]$$

in Cartesian coordinates, where **i**, **j**, **k** are unit vectors along $0x$, $0y$, $0z$. In terms of this operator, the grad, div and curl of an arbitrary scalar Ω and vector $\mathbf{F}(F_x, F_y, F_z)$ are:

$$\text{grad } \Omega = \nabla\Omega = \mathbf{i}\frac{\partial \Omega}{\partial x} + \mathbf{j}\frac{\partial \Omega}{\partial y} + \mathbf{k}\frac{\partial \Omega}{\partial z} \qquad [3.9]$$

$$\text{div } \mathbf{F} = \nabla.\mathbf{F} = \frac{\partial F_x}{\partial x} + \frac{\partial F_y}{\partial y} + \frac{\partial F_z}{\partial z} \qquad [3.10]$$

$$\text{curl } \mathbf{F} = \nabla \times \mathbf{F} = \begin{vmatrix} \mathbf{i} & \mathbf{j} & \mathbf{k} \\ \dfrac{\partial}{\partial x} & \dfrac{\partial}{\partial y} & \dfrac{\partial}{\partial z} \\ F_x & F_y & F_z \end{vmatrix} \qquad [3.11]$$

The square of the del operator, $\nabla^2 = \nabla.\nabla$, is a scalar operator of particular importance in electromagnetism, known as the *Laplacian*. Formally

$$\nabla^2 = \left(\mathbf{i}\frac{\partial}{\partial x} + \mathbf{j}\frac{\partial}{\partial y} + \mathbf{k}\frac{\partial}{\partial z}\right).\left(\mathbf{i}\frac{\partial}{\partial x} + \mathbf{j}\frac{\partial}{\partial y} + \mathbf{k}\frac{\partial}{\partial z}\right)$$

$$= \frac{\partial^2}{\partial x^2} + \frac{\partial^2}{\partial y^2} + \frac{\partial^2}{\partial z^2} \qquad [3.12]$$

and in terms of the vector operators,

$$\nabla^2 \Omega = \text{div (grad } \Omega). \qquad [3.13]$$

The scalar and vector fields resulting from the operations of ∇^2, grad, div and curl are here expressed in Cartesian coordinates, but their importance in vector analysis arises from their independence of any particular coordinate system. The latter can then be chosen according to the symmetry of the problem to which the differential equations are being applied.

For the electrostatic field, from equations [2.17] and [3.3] we have:

$$\nabla^2 \phi = \text{div (grad } \phi) = \text{div}(-\mathbf{E}) = -\rho/\epsilon_0. \qquad [3.14]$$

This is *Poisson's equation* for the electrostatic potential ϕ in the presence of an electric charge density ρ. It becomes *Laplace's equation*:

$$\nabla^2 \phi = 0 \qquad [3.15]$$

in the absence of any charges.

3.2 Solutions of Laplace's equation

The Laplacian operator in the spherical polar coordinates (r, θ, ψ) shown in Fig. 2.5 is:

$$\frac{1}{r^2}\frac{\partial}{\partial r}\left(r^2\frac{\partial}{\partial r}\right) + \frac{1}{r^2 \sin \theta}\frac{\partial}{\partial \theta}\left(\sin \theta \frac{\partial}{\partial \theta}\right) + \frac{1}{r^2 \sin \theta}\frac{\partial^2}{\partial \psi^2}. \qquad [3.16]$$

For the simplest solutions of Laplace's equation, let the electric potential ϕ be symmetrical about the polar axis so that $\partial\phi/\phi\psi = 0$. Then equations [3.15] and [3.16] give:

$$\frac{\partial}{\partial r}\left(r^2 \frac{\partial \phi}{\partial r}\right) + \frac{\partial}{\partial(\cos\theta)}\left\{(1 - \cos^2\theta)\frac{\partial \phi}{\partial(\cos\theta)}\right\} = 0.$$

For the highest symmetry ϕ is independent of θ or

$$\frac{\partial}{\partial r}\left(r^2 \frac{\partial \phi}{\partial r}\right) = 0$$

and it is obvious that $\phi_1 = r^{-1}$ is a solution, where for a sphere $r^2 = x^2 + y^2 + z^2$ in Cartesian coordinates. Since ϕ_1 is a solution of Laplace's equation, then so are partial derivatives of ϕ_1 with respect to the space coordinates, such as $\partial\phi_1/\partial x$, $\partial\phi_1/\partial z$. If the polar axis is $0z$ then $z = r\cos\theta$ (Fig. 2.5) and:

$$\frac{\partial\phi_1}{\partial z} = -\frac{1}{r^2}\cdot\frac{z}{r} = -\frac{z}{r^3} = -\frac{\cos\theta}{r^2}.$$

Hence $\phi_2 = r^{-2}\cos\theta$ is a solution and further solutions can be found by successive differentiation:

$$\frac{\partial\phi_2}{\partial z} = \frac{1}{r^3} - \frac{3}{r^4}\cdot\frac{z^2}{r} = \frac{1}{r^3}(1 - 3\cos^2\theta).$$

Thus $\phi_3 = r^{-3}(1 - 3\cos^2\theta)$ is a solution. In general it can be shown that the solutions are $\phi = r^n P_n$ and $\phi = r^{-(n+1)}P_n$, $n = 0, 1, 2 \ldots$ where P_n are *Legendre* functions. In electrostatics $\phi_1 = r^{-1}$ is just the spherically symmetric potential of a point charge (equation [2.13]), while $\phi_2 = r^{-2}\cos\theta$ is the potential at a distance $r \gg s$ for a dipole (equation [2.26] and exercise 1) and $\phi_3 = r^{-3}(1 - 3\cos^2\theta)$ is the long-range potential of a linear quadrupole (exercise 3).

These solutions can also be applied to such problems as a conducting sphere (exercise 5) or a dielectric sphere (exercise 6) in a uniform electric field. In each case the electric potentials can be used to obtain the electric fields from the polar components of grad ϕ:

$$(\text{grad }\phi)_r = \frac{\partial\phi}{\partial r} \quad \text{and} \quad (\text{grad }\phi)_\theta = \frac{1}{r}\frac{\partial\phi}{\partial\theta}. \qquad [3.17]$$

In cylindrical polar coordinates (r, θ, z) shown in Fig. 3.2, the Laplacian operator becomes:

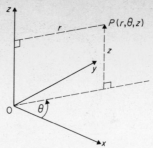

Fig. 3.2 Cylindrical polar coordinates (r, θ, z).

$$\frac{1}{r} \frac{\partial}{\partial r} \left(r \frac{\partial}{\partial r} \right) + \frac{1}{r^2} \frac{\partial^2}{\partial \theta^2} + \frac{\partial^2}{\partial z^2} \qquad [3.18]$$

but it is important to note that r is now normal to the z-axis and no longer a position vector from the origin. For a long coaxial cable the cylindrical symmetry produces a radial $\phi(r)$, except at the ends. Hence:

$$\nabla^2 \phi = \frac{1}{r} \frac{\partial}{\partial r} \left(r \frac{\partial}{\partial r} \right) \phi(r) = 0.$$

Since r is finite, on integration we obtain first:

$$r \frac{\partial \phi(r)}{\partial r} = A$$

and second:

$$\phi(r) = A \ln r + B \qquad [3.19]$$

where A and B are constants.

For the cross-section of the cable shown in Fig. 3.3, the usual arrangement is for the outer conductor of inner radius b to be earthed and the inner conductor of outer radius a to be at a potential V. Hence equation [3.19] becomes:

$$A \ln a + B = V$$

$$A \ln b + B = 0.$$

Subtracting

$$A \ln b/a = -V.$$

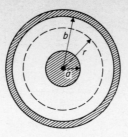

Fig. 3.3 Cross-section of a coaxial cable.

Hence [3.19] becomes:

$$\phi(r) = \frac{-V}{\ln(b/a)} \{\ln r - \ln b\} \qquad [3.20]$$

and the electric field

$$E_r = -\frac{\partial \phi}{\partial r} = \frac{-A}{r} = \frac{V}{r \ln(b/a)}.$$

This agrees with the solution obtained from Gauss's law (Chapter 2 and exercise 13).

In equation [3.20] the potential $\phi(r)$ is a solution of Laplace's equation that satisfies the boundary conditions of the problem and is valid for $a \leqslant r \leqslant b$. Since we found this function in a systematic manner by integration of Laplace's equation, we know that it is the only function with these properties. In many practical problems, with less symmetry, it is not usually possible to integrate Laplace's equation directly. Sometimes a solution can be found by intuition, sometimes by using an analogue method. An important theorem, the *uniqueness theorem* (proved in formal treatises), states that any potential that satisfies both Laplace's (or Poisson's) equation and the appropriate boundary conditions for a particular electric field is the *only possible* potential. This applies to any arrangement of conductors and dielectrics and so is very useful.

3.3 Electrical images

The uniqueness theorem enables the electric potentials and fields of charge distributions to be found by a substitutional technique known as the method of images. In this method, for example, a conductor is replaced by a point 'image' charge such that the conducting surface is still an equipotential surface. By the uniqueness theorem the electric potentials for a point charge plus its image are identical with those for a point charge and the conductor for the region *outside* the surface, since in both cases Laplace's equation is satisfied for all points outside the conductor. The method is illustrated by some examples here and exercises 8–10.

Point charge and plane conductor

A simple example is a point charge $+q$ near an earthed, infinite conducting plane (Fig. 3.4(a)). The charge will induce a surface

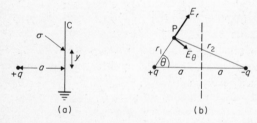

Fig. 3.4 (a) Point charge q at distance a from earthed conducting plane C induces surface charge density σ. (b) The image charge $-q$ at distance $2a$ from q replaces the conducting plane C.

density of charge σ on the conductor, which is related to the electric field E_0 just outside the surface by:

$$E_0 = \sigma/\epsilon_0 \tag{3.21}$$

as we showed from Fig. 2.13. At the conductor the electric field is everywhere normal to it and the problem is to find the electric field distribution and hence the distribution of the reduced charge on the conductor. In this case a charge $-q$ placed at the position of a virtual image of $+q$ in the conducting plane

(Fig. 3.4(b)) produces an equipotential surface (- - -) which is, like the conductor it replaces, at zero potential with respect to the two charges. Therefore the electric field produced at points such as P to the left of the zero potential surface by the charges $+q$ and $-q$ will be identical with that due to $+q$ and the earthed conductor, by the uniqueness theorem.

The potential ϕ at P(r, θ) is, from equation [2.13]:

$$\phi = \frac{1}{4\pi\epsilon_0}\left(\frac{q}{r_1} - \frac{q}{r_2}\right)$$

where, from Fig. 3.4(b):

$$r_2^2 = r_1^2 + 4a^2 - 4r_1 a \cos\theta.$$

The polar components of the electric field, are, from equations [2.17] and [3.17]:

$$E_r = -\frac{\partial\phi}{\partial r} = \frac{1}{4\pi\epsilon_0}\left\{\frac{q}{r_1^2} - \frac{q(r_1 - 2a\cos\theta)}{r_2^3}\right\} \qquad [3.22]$$

and $\quad E_\theta = -\frac{1}{r}\frac{\partial\phi}{\partial\theta} = -\frac{2qa\sin\theta}{4\pi\epsilon_0 r_2^3}.$ \qquad [3.23]

The electric field lines are plotted in Fig. 3.5, together with two sections of equipotential surfaces, which cut the field lines normally everywhere.

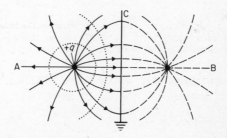

Fig. 3.5 Electric field lines ($\rightarrow$) from the charge q near the earthed conducting plane C. Sections through two equipotential surfaces are shown as dotted lines (. . .); the surfaces are generated by rotating these sections about AB. The imaginary field lines (- - -) of the image charge show the symmetry of the electric field lines, which are normal to the plane of C at all points on it.

The electric field at the surface of the conductor is everywhere normal to it and given by:

$$E_0 = E_r \cos\theta - E_\theta \sin\theta. \qquad [3.24]$$

At the surface $r_1 = r_2$ and E_0 points into the conductor, as the induced charges are negative. From equations [3.21] to [3.24]

$$E_0 = \frac{2qa}{4\pi\epsilon_0 r_1{}^3} = -\frac{\sigma}{\epsilon_0}$$

and so

$$\sigma = \frac{-qa}{2\pi r_1{}^3}$$

As a check, if we calculate the total charge induced on the conductor, from Fig. 3.4(a) we obtain:

$$\int_0^\infty \sigma 2\pi y \, \mathrm{d}y = -\frac{q}{2} \int_0^\infty \frac{a \, \mathrm{d}(y^2)}{(a^2 + y^2)^{3/2}} = -q$$

which is just the image charge we placed at $-x$. All image charges for conductors are, as in this case, virtual images, on the opposite side of the conductor to the inducing charge.

Having found the correct image charge, it is also possible to use it for other field calculations. For example, the conductor in this example attracts the charge $+q$ with the same Coulomb force as that between $+q$ and its image $-q$, that is $-q^2/(4\pi\epsilon_0.4a^2)$. The solution to this example (Fig. 3.5) may also be useful in finding the answer to a similar problem. For example, the equipotential surfaces in Fig. 3.5 could be curved conductors and so this solution would also give the electric field outside a curved conductor, of the appropriate shape, when a positive charge is brought near to it. The fields associated with a spherical conductor are discussed in exercises 9 and 10.

Point charge and plane dielectric

The problem of the electric field surrounding a point charge q_1 near a plane dielectric (Fig. 3.6(a)) is more complex than that for a conductor since the field penetrates the dielectric. In this case

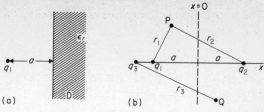

Fig. 3.6 (a) Point charge q_1 at distance a from plane dielectric D of relative permittivity ϵ_r. (b) The image charge q_2 at distance $2a$ from q_1 for fields outside the dielectric and the image charge q_3 for fields inside the dielectric replace the dielectric material.

two 'image' charges are suggested (Fig. 3.6(a)), q_2 at the virtual image position as before and q_3 outside the dielectric to represent the field inside. From Fig. 3.6(b), the potentials at P and Q are then:

$$\phi_P = \frac{1}{4\pi\epsilon_0} \left(\frac{q_1}{r_1} + \frac{q_2}{r_2} \right)$$

$$\phi_Q = \frac{q_3}{4\pi\epsilon_0 r_3}.$$

At the boundary $\phi_P = \phi_Q$ and, from equation [2.34], $E_{1t} = E_{2t}$. To satisfy these conditions we must have:

$$r_1 = r_2 = r_3$$

$$q_1 + q_2 = q_3. \tag{3.25}$$

Therefore q_3 coincides with q_1 and is the image of q_2 in the surface.

The other boundary condition, from equation [2.33], is $D_{1n} = D_{2n}$ or

$$\frac{\partial \phi_P}{\partial x} = \epsilon_r \frac{\partial \phi_Q}{\partial x}$$

since there is no free charge density at the surface of a dielectric. The analysis is essentially the same as in the previous example, the E_0 for a conductor becoming for the dielectric:

$$\frac{2a(q_1 - q_2)}{4\pi\epsilon_0 r_1^3} = \frac{\epsilon_r \cdot 2aq_3}{4\pi\epsilon_0 r_1^3}$$

and so:

$$q_1 - q_2 = \epsilon_r q_3. \tag{3.26}$$

The image charges, from equations [3.25] and [3.26] are therefore:

$$q_2 = -\left(\frac{\epsilon_r - 1}{\epsilon_r + 1}\right) q_1$$

$$q_3 = \frac{2}{(\epsilon_r + 1)} q_1$$

and the force of attraction of the charge q_1 to the dielectric is:

$$\frac{-q_1 q_2}{4\pi\epsilon_0 . 4a^2} = \frac{q_1^2 (\epsilon_r - 1)}{16\pi\epsilon_0 a^2 (\epsilon_r + 1)}.$$

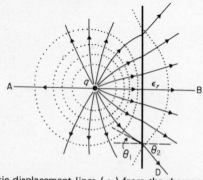

Fig. 3.7 Electric displacement lines ($\rightarrow$) from the charge q near the plane dielectric D of relative permittivity ϵ_r. Sections through two equipotential surfaces in the dielectric and three outside it are shown (. . .); their surfaces are generated by rotation about AB. Inside the dielectric the field lines are radial from q and the equipotential surfaces are spherical. At the boundary the field lines are refracted according to $\cot\theta_1 = \epsilon_r \cot\theta_2$.

In Fig. 3.7 the electric displacement **D** is described by the full lines and the equipotentials by the dotted lines. Inside the dielectric the electric field is due to the point charge q_3 and so is radial with spherical equipotential surfaces, but outside the induced surface charge superimposed on the point charge q_1 produces a complex field pattern. At the boundary, from equation [2.35]

$$\cot\theta_1 = \epsilon_r \cot\theta_2.$$

42 *Electric potential and fields*

3.4 Electron optics

In electronic instruments with visual displays, such as oscilloscopes or electron microscopes, it is necessary to focus beams of electrons in high vacua. In such cases the electrons are accelerated from an electron gun by voltages of the order of kilovolts and emerge at non-relativisitic speeds up to about $0.2c$. On the other hand for particle physics experiments, or to produce synchrotron radiation, electrons can be accelerated through gigavolts and the relativistic electron mass can be greater than that of a proton at rest. Electron optics is the study of electron trajectories over a wide range of speeds in vacuo and is a complex subject of great technical importance. Here only the principles of electrostatic lenses for non-relativistic electrons will be outlined, while magnetic lenses are described in the next chapter.

By analogy with geometrical optics, suppose we have a narrow beam of electrons travelling at velocity v_1 in an equipotential region at a potential of V_1 volts towards another equipotential region at a potential of V_2 volts (Fig. 3.8). At the boundary plane

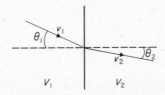

Fig. 3.8 Electrons at velocity v_1 in the equipotential region V_1 are refracted from an incident angle θ_1 to an emergent angle θ_2 at velocity v_2 in the equipotential region V_2.

there is a potential gradient, or electric field, that will accelerate the electrons normal to the boundary, but will not change their velocity parallel to the boundary. The emergent rays will be 'refracted' from an incident angle θ_1 to an angle θ_2 and their velocity v_2 will be given by:

$$v_1 \sin \theta_1 = v_2 \sin \theta_2.$$

But $\frac{1}{2}mv_1^2 = eV_1$

and $\frac{1}{2}mv_2{}^2 = eV_2$

so that

$$\frac{\sin \theta_1}{\sin \theta_2} = \frac{v_2}{v_1} = \sqrt{\frac{V_2}{V_1}}.$$

This is exactly analogous to Snell's law, $n_1 \sin \theta_1 = n_2 \sin \theta_2$, and we see that the electron velocity corresponds to the refractive index of the medium.

In a similar way since a convex lens focuses light, so a curved equipotential surface should focus electrons. Uniform electric fields (for example, Fig. 2.19) have plane equipotential surfaces associated with them, so we require non-uniform electric fields to focus electrons. A simple way to produce focusing is to have a single pair (Fig. 3.9(a)) or a double pair (Fig. 3.9(b)) of apertures,

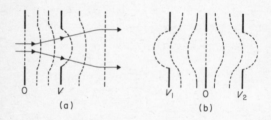

Fig. 3.9 Electric field lines (→) and equipotentials (– – –) for (a) a single pair and (b) a double pair of apertures.

each in a plane conductor. The field lines change smoothly from the high-field to the low-field region producing the required curved equipotentials. Another method is to have a gap between two cylindrical electrodes (Fig. 3.10). It is interesting to note that both an accelerating lens (Fig. 3.10(a)) and a decelerating lens (Fig. 3.10(b)) are net converging lenses, since in each case the electrons spend more time in the converging regions. However, these 'simple' electrostatic lenses are not simple optically, for they both accelerate the electrons horizontally and act on them through the radial component of the electric field.

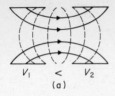 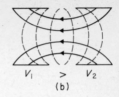

$$V_1 \; < \; V_2 \qquad\qquad V_1 \; > \; V_2$$
$$(a) \qquad\qquad\qquad\qquad (b)$$

Fig. 3.10 Electric field lines ($\rightarrow$) and equipotentials (- - -) for (a) an accelerating and (b) a decelerating cylindrical lens.

Thin electrostatic lens

In practice a lens of the type shown in Fig. 3.9(b) would have thick electrodes with rounded corners to avoid edge effects, as shown in Fig. 3.11(a). A system of this sort has cylindrical symmetry and so Laplace's equation in cylindrical polars, from equation [3.18], becomes:

$$\frac{1}{r} \frac{\partial}{\partial r} \left(r \frac{\partial \phi}{\partial r} \right) + \frac{\partial^2 \phi}{\partial z^2} = 0.$$

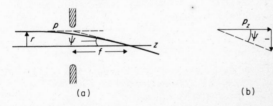

(a) (b)

Fig. 3.11 (a) Paraxial electron path through an aperture showing the focal length of the thin lens. (b) The axial and radial electron momenta.

Integrating

$$r \frac{\partial \phi}{\partial r} = - \int_0^r r \frac{\partial^2 \phi}{\partial z^2} \, dr = - \frac{r^2}{2} \frac{\partial^2 \phi}{\partial z^2}.$$

Thus

$$\frac{\partial \phi}{\partial r} = - \frac{r}{2} \frac{\partial^2 \phi}{\partial z^2}.$$

For electrons following paraxial trajectories, the axial velocity is $v_z = \mathrm{d}z/\mathrm{d}t$ at any point, while the radial momentum due to the radial force $e\partial\phi/\partial r$ on the electron is:

$$p_r = \int e \frac{\partial\phi}{\partial r}\,\mathrm{d}t = -\frac{er}{2}\int \frac{\partial^2\phi}{\partial z^2}\frac{\mathrm{d}z}{v_z}.$$

But the angle of deflection ψ of each electron is, from Fig. 3.11, given by:

$$\tan\psi = -\frac{p_r}{p_z} = -\frac{v_r}{v_z}$$

and, for paraxial rays, this is a small angle. We can therefore approximate v_z by the total speed $(2e\phi/m)^{\frac{1}{2}}$ at any point, so that:

$$p_r = -\frac{er}{2}\cdot\left(\frac{m}{2e}\right)^{\frac{1}{2}}\int \frac{\partial^2\phi}{\partial z^2}\cdot\frac{\mathrm{d}z}{\phi^{\frac{1}{2}}}.$$

This integral would be found numerically with a computer for a particular aperture and potential distribution, but it is evident that p_r is proportional to $-r$ for paraxial rays and so all the electrons with incident velocity parallel to the axis that pass through the aperture are brought to the same point on the axis. So there is a focus given by:

$$\tan\psi = -\frac{p_r}{p_z} = \frac{r}{f}.$$

The emergent focus for incident parallel rays from the central electrode in Fig. 3.9(b) is therefore:

$$\frac{1}{f_2} = \frac{\frac{1}{2}e\,(m/2e)^{\frac{1}{2}}}{(2eV_2 m)^{\frac{1}{2}}}\int \frac{\partial^2\phi}{\partial z^2}\frac{\mathrm{d}z}{\phi^{\frac{1}{2}}} = \frac{1}{4\sqrt{V_2}}\int \frac{\partial^2\phi}{\partial z^2}\frac{\mathrm{d}z}{\phi^{\frac{1}{2}}}.$$

A similar focus at $-f_1$ for electrons from the central electrode passing through V_1 (Fig. 3.9(b)), by symmetry, gives:

$$\frac{f_1}{f_2} = -\sqrt{\frac{V_1}{V_2}}$$

which is an exact analogy of the thin lens formula in geometrical optics with refractive indices n_1 and n_2 on each side.

Electric quadrupole lens

As in optics electron lenses may cause aberrations, so that finite apertures can produce spherical aberrations and, if the incident electrons are not monoenergetic, they can produce chromatic aberrations. Unlike photons, electrons repel one another and so an incident parallel beam slowly diverges producing an electronic aberration.

An example of an astigmatic electron lens is a combination of two quadrupole lenses with alternate potentials, the first producing a diverging focus and the second a converging focus. Quadrupole lenses have axial, but not cylindrical, symmetry, as shown in Fig. 3.12. Laplace's equation then reduces to:

$$\frac{\partial^2 \phi}{\partial x^2} + \frac{\partial^2 \phi}{\partial y^2} = 0$$

and ϕ is a two-dimensional potential, independent of the z-axis. In this example the equipotentials are $(x^2 - y^2)$ and the electric field lines from the hyperbolic conductors are $2xy$. As with the simple lens the electric field for an off-axis electron is proportional to the axial displacement (for example $-\partial \phi / \partial x = -2x$) and so produces a focus.

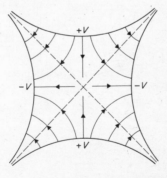

Fig. 3.12 Field lines (→) and hyperbolic conductors ($+V$, $-V$) form a cross-section of an electric quadrupole lens.

Chapter 4
Magnetostatics

Electrostatics has been the study of electric fields, electric potentials and electric forces due to charges at rest, i.e. stationary charges. These charges were of two types: free charges on conductors and fixed charges, arising from polarisation, on dielectrics. We concluded our study by considering how elecrostatic fields could be used to focus a diverging beam of electrons in a vacuum. In this chapter we first discuss the nature of a steady electric current I in matter and introduce the concept of the magnetic field **B**, sometimes called the magnetic induction field. The relationships between steady or magnetostatic fields having $\partial \mathbf{B}/\partial t = 0$ and steady or direct electric currents having $\partial I/\partial t = 0$ are then developed and illustrated with examples.

4.1 Electric current

What is an electric current? The simplest idea is to think of a stream of electrons in a vacuum (Fig. 4.1(a)). If there are N electrons per unit volume each of charge $-e$, then the charge density

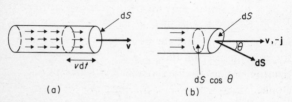

Fig. 4.1 (a) Electron stream in a vacuum. (b) Electric current is the flux of current density **j.dS**.

in the vacuum, $\rho = -Ne$. If they are all moving with the same velocity $\mathbf{v}$, then the charge flowing out of the area dS in time dt, where dS is normal to $\mathbf{v}$, is

$$dq = -Ne\,dS.\,v\,dt.$$

Therefore, the charge flowing out per second is

$$\frac{dq}{dt} = -Nev.\,dS.$$

We define a *current density* vector $\mathbf{j}$ as the positive charge flowing per unit area per second at a point and so

$$\frac{dq}{dt} = j\,dS$$

when $\mathbf{j}$, and hence $\mathbf{v}$, is normal to dS. Otherwise (Fig. 4.1(b)) we write:

$$\frac{dq}{dt} = -Ne\mathbf{v}.\mathbf{dS} = \mathbf{j}.\mathbf{dS}$$

where the scalar products $v\,dS\,\cos\theta$ and $j\,dS\,\cos\theta$ are similar to those found for the electric flux (Fig. 2.4). Hence

$$\mathbf{j} = -Ne\mathbf{v} = \rho\mathbf{v} \qquad\qquad [4.1]$$

for a stream of electrons, where $q = -e$. An electric current I is measured for a particular area S and is therefore

$$I = \int_S \mathbf{j}.\mathbf{dS} = \int \frac{dq}{dt}. \qquad\qquad [4.2]$$

Electric current is thus the flux of current density and has an SI unit 1 ampere equal to 1 coulomb per second, while current density is in amperes per square metre.

Of course, electric currents commonly travel in copper wires, so let us try and estimate an electric current from our definition for uniform electron flow, $I = jS = -NevS$. Copper has one free electron per atom and about 6×10^{23} atoms per mole with an atomic mass of 63 and density 9 $Mg\,m^{-3}$. Therefore, $N = 6 \times 10^{23} \times 9 \times 10^6/63 = 10^{29}\,m^{-3}$, $e = -1.6 \times 10^{-19}\,C$ and for a 1 mm diameter wire, $S \simeq 10^{-6}\,m^2$. But what is a reasonable value for v? We might think that since a short pulse travels down a 10 m cable in about 1 μs that $v = 10^7 \mathrm{m\,s^{-1}}$. Substituting this value, we get

$$I = 10^{29} \times 1.6 \times 10^{-19} \times 10^7 \times 10^{-6} \simeq 10^{11}\,\mathrm{A}!$$

This is many orders of magnitude too big for a typical current, so v must be much smaller. In fact, for a current of 1 A, v will be only $10^{-4}\,\mathrm{m\,s^{-1}}$. This is extremely slow: it would take an electron in such a current about *three hours* to travel 1 metre.

This simple estimate shows the drastic difference between electrons in a vacuum and 'free' electrons in a copper wire. A copper wire with no current flowing in it has a total charge that is zero; overall it is electrically neutral. An idea of its microscopic state is shown in Fig. 4.2(a): there are exactly the same

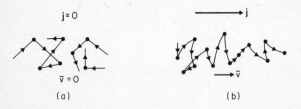

Fig. 4.2 Electron motion in a metal wire: (a) random, when there is no current flowing; (b) drifting in an electric current.

number of positive copper ions as there are 'free' negative electrons moving at random among them. When a constant electric field **E** is applied (Fig. 4.2(b)) each electron is accelerated during its free path by a force $-e\mathbf{E}$, but at each collision it loses its extra energy. The motion of the electrons through the wire is thus a diffusion process and we can associate a mean drift velocity $\bar{v}$ with this motion, which is just the acceleration times the mean time τ between collisions:

$$\bar{v} = \left(\frac{-eE}{m}\right)\tau \qquad [4.3]$$

where m is the electron mass. It is this drift velocity which we must use in equation [4.1] and not the much greater ($\sim 10^5\,\mathrm{m\,s^{-1}}$)

speed of the electrons between their random collisions, so that:

$$j = Ne^2 E\tau/m. \tag{4.4}$$

It is found experimentally for most materials that the relaxation time τ of the electrons is independent of the applied field E, but depends on such factors as the purity of the material and its temperature. We therefore define the *electrical conductivity* σ from the proportionality of j and E.

$$j = \sigma E \tag{4.5}$$

which is Ohm's law, with:

$$\sigma = Ne^2\tau/m \tag{4.6}$$

from equation [4.4]. The elementary form of the law follows for a uniform wire of cross-section S and length l having a voltage V applied to it. Since $I = jS$ from equation [4.2] and $E = V/l$,

$$I = \sigma \frac{V}{l} S = \frac{V}{R} \tag{4.7}$$

where $R = l/\sigma S$ is the *resistance* of the wire of conductivity σ. The SI units are ohm (Ω) for R and (ohm metre)$^{-1}$ or siemens per metre $(S\,m^{-1})$ for σ. Typical values of conductivity are given in Table 4.1, showing the wide choice available from high-conductivity metals through semiconductors to insulators.

From equation [4.6] we see that the behaviour of $\sigma(T)$ depends on the number density N and τ. In metals N is independent

Table 4.1 *Conductivity of materials at about 293 K*

Material	Conductivity $(S\,m^{-1})$
Copper	6.0×10^7
Silver	6.3×10^7
Lead	4.8×10^6
Mercury	1.0×10^6
Germanium	2.2
Silicon	1.8
Plate glass	3×10^{-11}
Mica	2×10^{-15}

of T and τ decreases as T rises, so that σ decreases with T rising. On the other hand, in semiconductors N increases as T rises, so that σ increases with rising T.

In a metal like copper it is easy to calculate the relaxation time τ from equation [4.6] using $\sigma = 6.0 \times 10^7 \, \text{S m}^{-1}$ and the answer, $\tau = 2 \times 10^{-14} \, \text{s}$, is an extremely short time. Since the conduction electrons in metals obey Fermi statistics, their random speed is their Fermi velocity, $v_F = 10^5 \, \text{m s}^{-1}$. They therefore travel about $\tau v_F = 2 \, \text{nm}$, or five lattice spacings, on average between collisions. In Table 4.2 the relative kinetic parameters for molecules in air at STP and for conduction electrons in copper at 293 K are compared. We see that the electron gas is much denser than air and the particles travel much faster, but they are scattered more frequently and so drift very slowly in a typical electric current.

Table 4.2 *Kinetic parameters for molecular and electron gases*

Parameter	Air molecules at STP	Copper electrons at 293 K	Units
Number density	4×10^{25}	10^{29}	m^{-3}
Typical drift velocity	1	10^{-4}	m s^{-1}
Relaxation time	2×10^{-10}	2×10^{-14}	s
Particle speed	500	10^5	m s^{-1}
Mean free path	100	2	nm

4.2 Lorentz force

Having established what we mean by an electric current, we proceed to investigate the effects of currents on one another and on electric charges. Experiments such as those of Ampère in 1820 showed (Fig. 4.3) that parallel currents in adjacent wires attract one another, while antiparallel currents repel. As shown in Chapter 1, the wires themselves are electrically neutral to a very high degree (about 1 in 10^{25}), so the force acting is not an electrostatic or Coulomb force. Further experiments have shown (Fig. 4.4) that there is no force acting between a stationary charge and a current, but charges moving parallel to a current

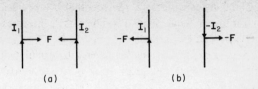

(a)   (b)

Fig. 4.3 Forces between currents: (a) parallel currents attract; (b) anti-parallel currents repel.

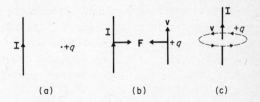

(a)   (b)   (c)

Fig. 4.4 Forces between a current and a charge. (a) No force for a stationary charge. (b) Attractive force for charge travelling parallel to the current. (c) No force for charge circulating in a plane normal to the current.

do attract it, while charges circulating round in a plane normal to the current produce no effect.

Exactly similar effects are found to be produced when currents are placed between the poles of a permanent magnet (Fig. 4.5): the currents are repelled out of the magnet in a direction

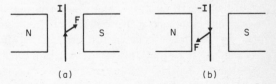

(a)   (b)

Fig. 4.5 Forces between a permanent magnet and a current: (a) current upwards, force inwards; (b) current downwards, force outwards.

depending on the direction of the current. Today we describe all these effects by attributing a *magnetic field* **B** to *both* the current in the wire *and* the (atomic) currents in the magnet. Experiments on charges q moving at a velocity **v** in the uniform field **B** of a magnet then show that the forces **F** shown in Fig. 4.3 to 4.5 can all be explained in terms of a new force acting on a moving charge in a magnetic field called the *Lorentz force*. This force is proportional to:

1. the charge q;
2. the speed v; and
3. the sine of the angle between **v** and **B**.

Furthermore it is always perpendicular to the plane containing **v** and **B**. It is given by:

$$\mathbf{F} \propto q\mathbf{v} \times \mathbf{B}$$

and illustrated in Fig. 4.6. In the SI system the constant of proportionality is unity and this equation can be used to define the

Fig. 4.6 The Lorentz force **F** on a charge with velocity **v** in a uniform magnetic field **B**. (a) A large force. (b) A small force.

unit of magnetic field **B**: one tesla is that magnetic field which produces a force of 1 newton on a charge of 1 coulomb moving at 1 metre per second normal to the field. Therefore in SI units,

$$\mathbf{F} = q\mathbf{v} \times \mathbf{B}. \tag{4.8}$$

Magnetic fields produced by powerful superconducting solenoids can be 10 tesla or more. These are huge when compared with the earth's magnetic field (about 100 microtesla), but dwarfed by the microscopic fields near nuclei which can be 10 kilotesla. An older unit of **B**, the gauss, is still sometimes used; 1 tesla is exactly equal to 10 kilogauss.

In the presence of both an electric field and a magnetic field, the total force on a charge q is the sum of the Coulomb and Lorentz forces:

$$\mathbf{F} = q\mathbf{E} + q\mathbf{v} \times \mathbf{B}. \tag{4.9}$$

This is not immediately obvious, for Coulomb's force described the interaction of stationary charges. It is one of the remarkable properties of electric charge that it is invariant at all speeds, even relativistic ones, so that equation [4.9] is always true.

Applications to charged particles

The Lorentz force law is used to find the trajectories of charged particles moving in steady magnetic fields. We shall now look at some typical examples.

1. *Circular motion*

When a charged particle enters a uniform magnetic field **B** with a velocity **v** in the plane normal to **B**, the force **F** = q**v** X **B** is constant and always normal to the motion. Therefore the trajectory is a circle of radius R (Fig. 4.7(a)) given by:

$$F = \frac{mv^2}{R} = q\,v\,B$$

or $\quad R = \frac{mv}{qB}.$ [4.10]

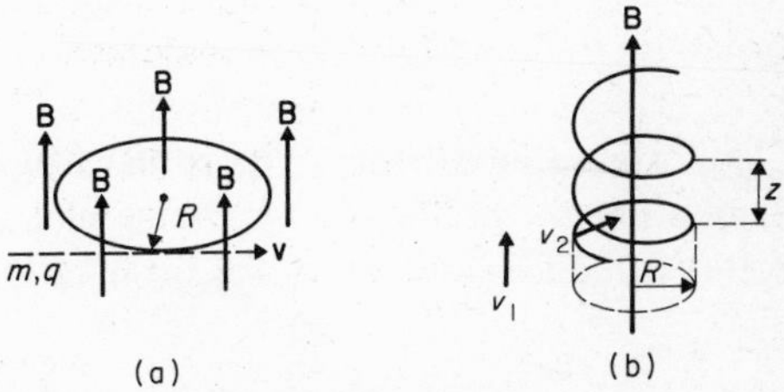

(a)   (b)

Fig. 4.7 Motion of a charged particle in a uniform magnetic field **B**. (a) Enters field in plane normal to **B**. (b) Enters at another angle to **B**.

2. *Helical motion*

If the charged particle enters a uniform field **B** at any other angle, then we resolve **v** into v_1 parallel to **B** and v_2 normal to **B** (Fig. 4.7(b)). The speed parallel to **B** is not affected, while the speed normal to **B** would produce circular motion of radius **R** = mv_2/qB. The total motion is therefore a helix around **B** of pitch $z = 2\pi m v_1/qB$.

3. *Magnetic quadrupole lens*

Non-uniform magnetic fields are used to focus beams of charged particles and so constitute magnetic lenses in television sets and particle accelerators. An arrangement of pole pieces similar to that of the electric quadrupole lens (Fig. 3.12) forms a magnetic quadrupole lens (Fig. 4.8(a)). It can be shown that

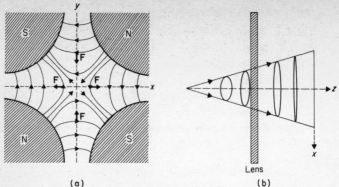

Fig. 4.8 (a) Magnetic field lines (→) and shaped pole pieces form a cross-section of a magnetic quadrupole lens. (b) The lens focuses a cone of electrons to a horizontal line.

(a)   (b)

an electron entering this magnetic field near the z-axis is deflected by the forces **F** to keep it in the horizontal xz plane. The effect on a cone of electrons is shown in Fig. 4.8(b) for this lens, while a similar lens with each polarity reversed would produce a line focus along $0y$. A pair of quadrupole lenses can therefore produce a point focus from a diverging beam.

Applications to electric currents

The Lorentz force law can also be used to investigate the motion of current carrying coils in magnetic fields.

1. *Current loop*

A coil carrying a current experiences a torque when placed in a uniform magnetic field due to the Lorentz forces acting on it. From Fig. 4.9(a) the current in side bc of the coil is, using equation [4.2],

$$\mathbf{I} = -Ne\mathbf{v}A$$

where A is the cross-sectional area of the wire and $\mathbf{v}$ is the drift velocity of the electrons of number density N. The Lorentz force acts on all these electrons and so is:

$$\mathbf{F}_1 = -(NAL_1)\,e\mathbf{v} \times \mathbf{B} \tag{4.11}$$

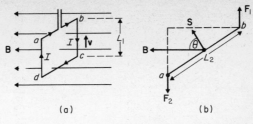

Fig. 4.9 A torque acts on a current loop in a magnetic field (a) Side view. (b) Plan.

with magnitude $F_1 = L_1 IB$, and direction shown in Fig. 4.9(b). Similarly for *ad*, $F_2 = L_1 IB$, but acting in the opposite direction. Another similar couple acts in the vertical plane on the sides *ab* and *dc*. The net force acting to displace the coil is therefore zero, but if the plane of the coil is not normal to **B** there will be a torque acting to rotate the coil into this position of magnitude:

$$T = F_1 L_z \sin\theta = IL_1 L_2 B \sin\theta$$

where θ is the angle, shown in Fig. 4.9(b), between the normal $\hat{\mathbf{n}}$ to the plane of the coil and **B**. If **S** is the vector area $L_1 L_2 \hat{\mathbf{n}}$, then the torque is:

$$\mathbf{T} = I\mathbf{S} \times \mathbf{B}.$$

For a small coil of arbitrary shape and area d*S*, known as a *current loop*, this equation is still true. For such a current loop we define the *magnetic dipole moment* by:

$$\mathbf{m} = I\mathbf{dS} \qquad\qquad [4.12]$$

where the vector **dS** points in the direction given by applying the right-hand screw rule to the direction of the current. The SI unit of magnetic moment is therefore $\mathrm{A\,m^2}$ and the torque on a current loop in a uniform field is:

$$\mathbf{T} = \mathbf{m} \times \mathbf{B}. \qquad\qquad [4.13]$$

A similar torque $\mathbf{p} \times \mathbf{E}$ can be shown to act on an electric dipole in a uniform electric field (exercise 4, chapter 3).

2. Current element

A short length dl of a wire carrying a current I is called a *current element*. The direction of the current is indicated by the vector length **dl**, which is always in the opposite direction to the drift velocity of the electrons **v**. The force on a current element is, from equation [4.11],

$$\mathbf{dF} = -(Na\,dl)\,e\mathbf{v} \times \mathbf{B}$$

or $\quad \mathbf{dF} = +(NAev)\,\mathbf{dl} \times \mathbf{B}$.

The magnitude of the current $I = NAev$, therefore

$$\mathbf{dF} = I\mathbf{dl} \times \mathbf{B}. \qquad [4.14]$$

This is an important extension of the Lorentz force law to current elements, which will enable us to obtain the force between steady currents, when we know the magnetic field due to a current element.

4.3 Biot–Savart law

In Chapter 2 we showed how to calculate the electric field at a point 1 (Fig. 4.10(a)) due to a charge density distribution. We obtained equation [2.5],

$$\mathbf{E}(1) = \frac{1}{4\pi\epsilon_0} \int_{\substack{\text{all} \\ \text{space}}} \frac{\rho(2)\,\hat{\mathbf{r}}_{12}}{r_{12}^2} \, d\tau_2$$

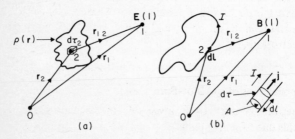

Fig. 4.10 (a) The electric field **E**(1) due to a distribution of charge. (b) The magnetic field **B**(1) due to a current.

where $\rho(2)$ was the charge density at point 2 and $\int d\tau$ was a triple integral over all space. This was based on Coulomb's law and the principle of superposition of electric fields.

In magnetostatics there is a similar integral which relates the magnetic field at a point 1 (Fig. 4.10(b)) due to the current in a circuit by integrating over the complete circuit. It is more complicated than the electrostatic case because it depends on moving charges and that implies a vector current density $\mathbf{j}(2)$ and a vector product between $\mathbf{j}(2)$ and $\hat{\mathbf{r}}_{12}$. The equation is:

$$\mathbf{B}(1) = \frac{\mu_0}{4\pi} \int_{\substack{\text{all} \\ \text{space}}} \frac{\mathbf{j}(2) \times \hat{\mathbf{r}}_{12}}{r_{12}^2} \, d\tau_2 \qquad [4.15]$$

where the *magnetic constant*

$$\mu_0 = \frac{1}{\epsilon_0 c^2} = 4\pi \times 10^{-7} \, \text{N A}^{-2} \qquad [4.16]$$

from equation [2.2].

If the circuit is composed of thin wires, then we can write

$$\mathbf{j}d\tau = \mathbf{j}A \, dl = I\mathbf{dl}$$

where $\mathbf{dl}$ is the vector length of a current element in the same direction as $\mathbf{j}$. Hence equation [4.15] becomes:

$$\mathbf{B}(1) = \frac{\mu_0}{4\pi} \oint \frac{I\mathbf{dl} \times \hat{\mathbf{r}}_{12}}{r_{12}^2} \qquad [4.17]$$

where the integral is taken all round the circuit. This is the law named after Biot and Savart who, with Ampère, showed that it fitted the results of several experiments undertaken around 1820. Its status in magnetostatics is similar to that of Coulomb's law in electrostatics.

Applications of the Biot–Savart law

The Biot–Savart law is invaluable in calculating the magnetic fields due to simple circuits.

1. *Infinite wire*

The magnitude of **B** due to an infinite wire carrying current I is, at point P (Fig. 4.11(a)):

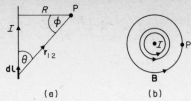

(a)   (b)

Fig. 4.11 The magnetic field due to an infinite wire at P. (a) Side view of current. (b) Plan of the field lines.

$$B = \frac{\mu_0}{4\pi} \int_{-\infty}^{+\infty} \frac{I dl \sin\theta}{r_{12}^2}.$$

To evaluate this integral, we note that the perpendicular distance R is fixed, that $r_{12} = R/\cos\phi$, $\sin\theta = \cos\phi$ and $l = R\tan\phi$. Hence the integral becomes:

$$B = \frac{\mu_0 I}{4\pi} \int_{-\pi/2}^{\pi/2} R\sec^2\phi \, d\phi \cos\phi . \frac{\cos^2\phi}{R^2}$$

and $$B = \frac{\mu_0 I}{4R} \left[\sin\phi\right]_{-\pi/2}^{\pi/2} = \frac{\mu_0 I}{2\pi R}.$$ [4.18]

The direction of **B** is given by the right-hand screw rule for the vector product **dl** $\times$ **r**$_{12}$ and so is into the paper at P. Combining these results we see that **B** forms concentric circular field lines in planes normal to the wire (Fig. 4.11(b)) and falls off as $1/R$.

2. *Current loop*

A circular current around the origin in the xy plane (Fig. 4.12) produces a field **dB** normal to each current element I**dl** and each distance vector **r**$_{12}$. By symmetry the total **B** will be along the z-axis and be:

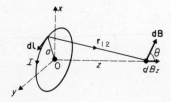

Fig. 4.12 Magnetic field on axis of a current loop.

$$B = \oint dB_z = \frac{\mu_0}{4\pi} \oint \frac{I dl \cos\theta}{r_{12}^2}.$$

But $\cos\theta = a/r_{12} = a/(a^2 + z^2)^{\frac{1}{2}}$ is a constant and $\oint dl = 2\pi a$, so that

$$B = \frac{\mu_0 I a^2}{2(a^2 + z^2)^{3/2}}.$$

The direction of **B** is towards you when you look into an anti-clockwise (positive) current.

At the centre of the loop **B** has a maximum amplitude of $\mu_0 I / 2a$, while at a large distance $z \gg a$,

$$B = \frac{\mu_0 I a^2}{2z^3} = \frac{\mu_0}{4\pi} \frac{2m}{z^3} \qquad [4.19]$$

where $m = I\pi a^2$ is the magnetic dipole moment. Thus the field of a current loop at long range falls off as $1/z^3$ in a similar way to that of an electric dipole (exercise 1, chapter 3).

4.4 Forces between currents

We can now combine equation [4.14], the Lorentz force law for current elements, with the Biot-Savart law equation [4.17] to obtain the forces between two current elements. In general (Fig. 4.13(a)) we have:

$$d\mathbf{B}_1 = \frac{\mu_0}{4\pi} \left(\frac{I_2 d\mathbf{l}_2 \times \hat{\mathbf{r}}_{12}}{r_{12}^2} \right)$$

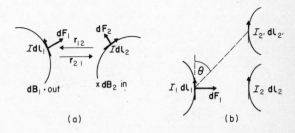

Fig. 4.13 Forces between currents: (a) random orientation; (b) parallel.

and therefore from equation [4.14]

$$dF_1 = \frac{\mu_0}{4\pi} \left\{ \frac{I_1 dl_1 \times (I_2 dl_2 \times \hat{r}_{12})}{r_{12}^2} \right\} \qquad [4.20]$$

and similarly

$$dF_2 = \frac{\mu_0}{4\pi} \left\{ \frac{I_2 dl_2 \times (I_1 dl_1 \times \hat{r}_{21})}{r_{12}^2} \right\}. \qquad [4.21]$$

The directions of the magnetic fields and forces are shown in the figure and clearly $dF_1 = dF_2$ in magnitude but not in direction.

We note that the forces are attractive, as was shown in experiments on parallel currents (Fig. 4.3(a)), and that there is apparently a net upward force when the wires are not parallel. However, there is no violation of Newton's third law, since on integrating these equations to get the total net force on a circuit the result is zero. For the simpler case of parallel wires (Fig. 4.13(b)), we obtain:

$$dF_1 = \frac{\mu_0 I_1 dl_1 I_2 dl_2 \sin \theta}{4\pi r_{12}^2}$$

when the current elements are displaced by an angle θ and

$$dF_1 = \frac{\mu_0 I_1 I_2 dl_1 dl_2}{4\pi r_{12}^2} \qquad [4.22]$$

when they are adjacent. The complexity of equations [4.20] and [4.21] arises directly from the Lorentz force law, and the apparent simplicity of equation [4.22] is due to the high symmetry of adjacent, parallel current elements.

The force between two currents is used in establishing the fourth base unit of the International System of Units (SI), that is the ampere: 'The ampere is that constant current which, if maintained in two straight parallel conductors of infinite length, of negligible circular cross-section, and placed 1 metre apart in vacuum, would produce between these conductors a force equal to 2×10^{-7} newton per metre of length'. This follows from equations [4.14], [4.16] and [4.18], which give the force per unit length required as:

$$I \cdot \frac{\mu_0 I}{2\pi R} = 2 \times 10^{-7} \frac{I^2}{R}.$$

4.5 Ampère's law and magnetic flux

In magnetostatics the circulation law corresponding to $\oint_C \mathbf{E}.\mathbf{ds} = 0$ in electrostatics is known as Ampère's law and enables us to find $\oint_C \mathbf{B}.\mathbf{ds}$. In general it is not zero and so $\mathbf{B}$ is *not* normally a conservative field, derivable from a scalar, magnetostatic potential. A simple example shows this to be true: the field lines around an infinite wire carrying a current I (Fig. 4.11) are circles in the planes normal to the wire. So if we evaluate $\oint_C \mathbf{B}.\mathbf{ds}$ around a circular path distance R from the wire, using equation [4.18] for $\mathbf{B}$, we have:

$$\oint_C \mathbf{B}.\mathbf{ds} = \frac{\mu_0 I}{2\pi R} \oint_C \mathrm{d}s = \mu_0 I. \qquad [4.23]$$

However, it is not necessary to choose a circular path for the contour, as Fig. 4.14 makes clear. Any irregular contour can be

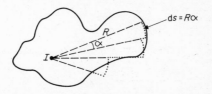

Fig. 4.14 Ampère's law applied to an irregular contour.

approximated by small arcs $\mathrm{d}s = R\alpha$ plus radials, for each radial $\mathbf{B}$ due to I is normal to the radius vector and so

$$\oint_{\text{radials}} \mathbf{B}.\mathbf{ds} = 0.$$

On the other hand, for each arc $\mathbf{B}$ is proportional to $1/R$ and so $\mathbf{B}.\mathbf{ds}$ depends only on the angles α. Therefore:

$$\oint_C \mathbf{B}.\mathbf{ds} = \oint_{\text{arcs}} \mathbf{B}.\mathbf{ds} = \frac{\mu_0 I}{2\pi} \oint \alpha = \mu_0 I.$$

Of course if $\oint_C \mathbf{B}.\mathbf{ds}$ does not enclose any currents, then

$$\oint_C \mathbf{B}.\mathbf{ds} = 0$$

as in the electrostatic case. In general there will be contributions from each current enclosed, which in turn are given by equation [4.2], so that:

$$\oint_C \mathbf{B}.\mathbf{ds} = \mu_0 \int_S \mathbf{j}.\mathbf{dS}. \qquad [4.24]$$

This is *Ampère's law*: the circulation of $\mathbf{B}$ is μ_0 times the current density flux enclosed.

Applications of Ampère's law

Ampère's law (equations [4.23] or [4.24]) is useful in obtaining the magnetic field of large, symmetrical circuits.

1. *Torus*

A torus (Fig. 4.15(a)) of N turns each carrying a current I has a uniform magnetic field B at the centre of each turn (Fig. 4.15(b)) and so a suitable Ampèrian contour is the

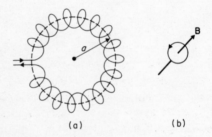

(a) (b)

Fig. 4.15 (a) Ampèrian contour for a torus. (b) Magnetic field of each turn.

circular axis of the torus. For this contour the currents on the inside thread the circle, while those on the outside do not. Therefore

$$\oint_C \mathbf{B}.\mathbf{ds} = \mu_0 N I$$

from which

$$B = \frac{\mu_0 N I}{2\pi a}. \qquad [4.25]$$

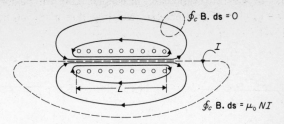

$$\oint_c \mathbf{B . ds} = 0$$

$$\oint_c \mathbf{B . ds} = \mu_0 NI$$

Fig. 4.16 Magnetic field lines and Ampèrian contours for a long solenoid.

2. Solenoid

If we ignore the diverging fields at the ends of the solenoid, then the uniform field **B** inside the solenoid can be found from Ampère's law. In Fig. 4.16 it is obvious that the large contour contains the current in each turn once and integrates the uniform field **B** over the length L of the solenoid. Therefore:

$$\oint_C \mathbf{B . ds} = BL = \mu_0 NI \qquad [4.26]$$

and $B = \mu_0 nI \qquad [4.27]$

where n is the number of turns per unit length. On the other hand a contour that does not enclose a current has zero circulation and so cannot be used to find **B** external to the solenoid. It is important to note that the field lines of **B** are always closed loops with no beginning or end point: this is because magnetic monopoles do not exist (compare Fig. 4.16 and 2.19). (Recent theories of elementary particles imply that magnetic monopoles should exist in certain circumstances and so experimenters are trying to detect these rare particles.)

Magnetic flux

We define *magnetic flux* Φ as $\int_S \mathbf{B . dS}$, by analogy with the electric flux of Gauss's law. The SI unit of magnetic flux is the weber (Wb) and so the unit of magnetic field (or flux density) is sometimes taken as Wb m^{-2} rather than tesla. For any closed surface S

$$\Phi = \int_S \mathbf{B} \cdot d\mathbf{S} = 0 \qquad\qquad [4.28]$$

since there are no magnetic monopoles to make the total flux finite. This is *Gauss's law* for magnetism.

The concept of magnetic flux is mainly used for surfaces that are not closed, as illustrated in Fig. 4.17 for uniform and non-uniform fields. The *flux linkage* for a circuit of N turns is $N\Phi$ in each case.

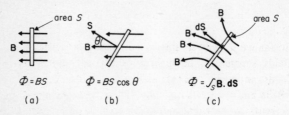

Fig. 4.17 Magnetic flux for: (a) coils normal to **B**; (b) coil at angle θ to **B**; and (c) non-uniform **B**.

Applying Gauss's divergence theorem (equation [3.2]) to Gauss's law for magnetostatics (equation [4.28]), we see that:

$$\int_S \mathbf{B} \cdot d\mathbf{S} = \int_V \text{div } \mathbf{B} d\tau = 0.$$

Therefore

$$\text{div } \mathbf{B} = 0 \qquad\qquad [4.29]$$

and we see that **B** is always a divergence free field. Since this is due to the absence of magnetic monopoles, it is always true.

Chapter 5
Electromagnetism

So far we have been able to consider electric fields and magnetic fields separately, through imposing the conditions that these fields and any currents shall be in steady states with $\partial \mathbf{E}/\partial t$, $\partial \mathbf{B}/\partial t$ and $\partial \mathbf{j}/\partial t$ all zero. In this chapter we move from steady currents to varying currents, from steady electric fields to induced electric fields, from stationary to moving circuits. Electric and magnetic effects become intimately connected in the study of electromagnetism, which has already been introduced in the electromagnetic force equation [4.9]:

$$\mathbf{F} = q\mathbf{E} + q\mathbf{v} \times \mathbf{B}.$$

We first develop the concepts contained in Faraday's law and then apply it to a variety of examples.

5.1 Faraday's law

In a series of experiments in 1831–2 Faraday showed conclusively that electricity from batteries and magnetism from iron magnets were not separate phenomena but intimately related. He discovered that voltages can be generated in a circuit in three different ways:

1. by moving the circuit in a magnetic field;
2. by moving a magnet near the circuit; and
3. by changing the current in an adjacent circuit.

Consider the simple system shown in Fig. 5.1: a solenoid producing an axial field **B** which passes through a current loop connected to a galvanometer (current detector). The galvanometer needle kicks if:

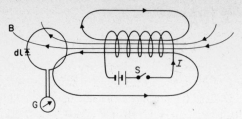

Fig. 5.1 A solenoid produces a magnetic field **B**, which is sensed by a current loop and a galvanometer G.

1. the solenoid is moved backwards and forwards;
2. the current loop is moved;
3. the current in the solenoid is switched on or off without moving any circuits.

The needle only moves when there is a current in the loop, i.e. when there is a net force on the electrons in the wire in one direction along it. There may be several different forces acting on different parts of the loop but what moves the needle is the net force integrated around the complete circuit. This is the *electromotive force* (e.m.f.)

$$\mathscr{E} = \oint \frac{\mathbf{F}}{q} . \, d\mathbf{l} = \oint \mathbf{E} . \, d\mathbf{l} \qquad [5.1]$$

where **F** is the force on charge q and the integral is taken round the loop. The definition of $\mathscr{E}$ is therefore the tangential force per unit charge in the wire integrated over the complete circuit.

We can illustrate this definition by considering the work done by a battery of e.m.f. $\mathscr{E}$ driving a charge q around a circuit (Fig. 5.2). The work done by the battery is $\mathscr{E}q$, while that done on the charge in moving a distance **dl** is **F.dl**. Therefore

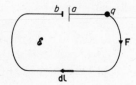

Fig. 5.2 A battery of e.m.f. $\mathscr{E}$ drives a charge q around a circuit.

$$\mathcal{E}q = \int_a^b \mathbf{F}.\mathbf{dl}$$

and
$$\mathcal{E} = \int_a^b \frac{\mathbf{F}}{q}.\mathbf{dl} = \int_a^b \mathbf{E}.\mathbf{dl}$$

where $\mathbf{E} = \mathbf{F}/q$ is the electric field or force per unit charge. The SI units for $\mathcal{E}$ and $\mathbf{E}$ are obviously not the same: e.m.f. is measured in volts, electric field in volts per metre.

Motional e.m.f.s

The concept of electromotive force generated by the motion of circuits is best understood by considering some examples.

1. *Metal rod in a uniform field*

In Fig. 5.3 a metal rod AB of length L is placed on the y-axis and moved along $0x$ in the uniform magnetic field $\mathbf{B}$ in the z-direction. By the Lorentz force law, each electron in the wire

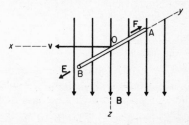

Fig. 5.3 A metal rod moves in a uniform magnetic field.

experiences a force $\mathbf{F} = -e\mathbf{v} \times \mathbf{B}$ and so the free electrons tend to move towards A. This produces a distribution of excess negative charge, which by Gauss's law is equivalent to an electric field $\mathbf{E}$ and so a net force $-e\mathbf{E}$ on each electron. Therefore

$$\mathbf{E} = \mathbf{v} \times \mathbf{B}. \tag{5.2}$$

From equation [5.1] the total e.m.f. across the rod will be:

$$\mathcal{E}_{AB} = \int_B^A \mathbf{E}.\mathbf{dy} = v_x B_z L.$$

This e.m.f. is due to the electric field **E** induced in the rod by its motion through the operation of the Lorentz force law.

2. *Metal rod on rails in a uniform field*

In Fig. 5.4 the same metal rod AB is mounted on metal rails so that a circuit ABCD of variable size is formed as the rod moves.

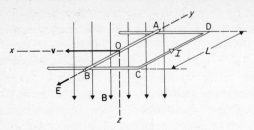

Fig. 5.4 A metal rod moving in a uniform magnetic field generates a current in a circuit.

The electrons now drift from B to A and go round DCB to form a conventional current I in the opposite direction. The e.m.f. generated by the rod moving is unchanged, but it now produces a current:

$$I = \frac{v_x B_z L}{R}$$

where R is the total resistance of the circuit ABCD.

3. *Current loop in a uniform field*

In Fig. 5.5 a square current loop abcd is moving into and out of a uniform magnetic field **B**. If the sides of the loop are parallel to 0x and 0y and **B** is in the z direction, then motion

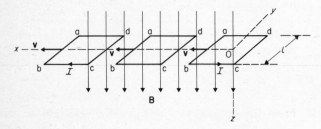

Fig. 5.5 A current loop moves in a uniform magnetic field.

at velocity **v** along 0x will produce an e.m.f. & along ab as it enters the field. This will generate a current $I = v_x B_z l/r$, where l is the length ab and r is the resistance of the loop, until the side cd enters the field. Then an e.m.f. & will be generated in dc and this will exactly cancel that in ab giving zero current. Finally as it emerges from the field there will only be the e.m.f. & in dc and this will generate I in the opposite direction in the loop.

The source of this electrical energy is the mechanical work done in moving the coil. It is dissipated in the loop as heat, which by Joule's law is $I^2 r$ watts. The mechanical work can equally well be done by moving the magnetic field across a stationary loop: it is essentially a relative motion effect. An observer on the coil in this case would see a moving magnetic field $\mathbf{B}(t)$ and would ascribe the current to a moving electric field $\mathbf{E}(t)$. In terms of magnetic flux, at any instant the flux through the coil

$$\Phi = B_z lx$$

and so:

$$\left| \text{&} \right| = v_x B_z l = \frac{\mathrm{d}x}{\mathrm{d}t} B_z l = \frac{\mathrm{d}\Phi}{\mathrm{d}t}. \qquad [5.3]$$

This equation is an expression of the '*flux rule*' found experimentally by Faraday: an e.m.f. is induced in a circuit whenever the flux through it changes from any cause. The *direction* of the e.m.f. was established by Lenz and is known as *Lenz's law*: the current induced tends to oppose the change of flux through the circuit. The combination of the flux rule and Lenz's law is known as *Faraday's law*: the e.m.f. induced in a circuit is equal to the negative rate of change of the magnetic flux through that circuit. That is:

$$\text{&} = \oint \mathbf{E.dl} = -\frac{\mathrm{d}\Phi}{\mathrm{d}t}. \qquad [5.4]$$

From the definition of magnetic flux this can be written:

$$\oint \mathbf{E.dl} = -\frac{\mathrm{d}}{\mathrm{d}t} \int_S \mathbf{B.dS}. \qquad [5.5]$$

Here the direction of the vectors **dS** are given by the right-hand screw rule for the circulation around S in the line integral.

Clearly the induced electric field in equation [5.5] is not an electrostatic field, for which the circulation law gives $\oint \mathbf{E}.d\mathbf{l} = 0$, but arises from the Lorentz force $q\mathbf{v} \times \mathbf{B}$ in the case of motional e.m.f.s and from dB/dt when the magnetic field is varying. These can be different phenomena, although both are represented by Faraday's law. It is therefore important to distinguish between them.

Motional and transformer e.m.f.s

We can summarise the results on *motional e.m.f.s* by

$$\oint \mathbf{E}.d\mathbf{l} = \oint (\mathbf{v} \times \mathbf{B}).d\mathbf{l} \qquad [5.6]$$

where **v** is the relative motion of a circuit with respect to the frame (usually the laboratory frame) in which **B** is fixed. We say that the circuit, which must not be changing in its shape or composition, is cutting the magnetic flux. This is true whether **B** is a steady magnetic field or a time-varying magnetic field.

The *transformer e.m.f.s* arise when there is no motion and **E** and **B** are fixed in the same coordinate system, so that:

$$\oint \mathbf{E}.d\mathbf{l} = -\frac{d}{dt} \int_S \mathbf{B}.d\mathbf{S} = - \int_S \frac{\partial \mathbf{B}}{\partial t}.d\mathbf{S} \qquad [5.7]$$

where the induced field **E** is due solely to the time variation of the magnetic field **B** and is therefore zero for a steady field. The time derivative now refers to each elementary area separately and so is a partial derivative. Now there is no longer any flux cutting and so there is no need to restrict the line integral to a circuit. It can be any contour in space and equation [5.7] becomes:

$$\oint_C \mathbf{E}.d\mathbf{s} = - \int_S \frac{\partial \mathbf{B}}{\partial t}.d\mathbf{S}. \qquad [5.8]$$

Combining this with Stokes's theorem (equation [3.6]), we obtain the differential form of Faraday's law:

$$\text{curl } \mathbf{E} = -\frac{\partial \mathbf{B}}{\partial t}. \qquad [5.9]$$

This is always true, giving as its time-independent limit the circulation law of the electrostatic field, curl **E** = 0. Equation [5.9] and the electromagnetic force equation [4.9] are the two fundamental equations of electromagnetism.

5.2 Applications of Faraday's law

We will now illustrate the usefulness of Faraday's law, as expressed in equations [5.4], [5.6] and [5.8].

Betatron

The betatron is a circular electron accelerator (Fig. 5.6) with the electrons circulating in a vacuum chamber placed in a powerful,

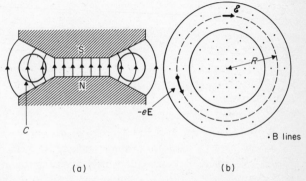

(a) (b)

Fig. 5.6 The betatron. (a) Vertical section through the magnet NS and vacuum chamber C. (b) Top view of central section of the vacuum chamber.

non-uniform magnetic field produced by shaped pole-pieces. The electrons are accelerated by increasing the magnetic field, which generates an e.m.f. in the vacuum given by:

$$\mathcal{E} = \oint_C \mathbf{E} . \mathbf{ds} = - \int_S \frac{\partial \mathbf{B}}{\partial t} . \mathbf{dS}. \qquad [5.10]$$

If we assume the electrons are injected into an orbit radius R for which the mean field is $\bar{B}$, then equation [5.10] becomes:

$$2\pi RE = -\frac{d\bar{B}}{dt} . \pi R^2$$

or $\quad E = -\frac{R}{2}\frac{d\bar{B}}{dt}.$

The e.m.f. generated opposes the increasing magnetic flux and so its direction is clockwise when viewed from above the magnet (Fig. 5.6(b)) and therefore the electron motion is anticlockwise when driven by the force $-e\mathbf{E}$. The rate of change of momentum p of the electron is therefore:

$$\frac{dp}{dt} = -eE = \frac{eR}{2}\frac{d\bar{B}}{dt}.$$

But we have already seen (equation [4.10]) that the momentum of an electron in a circular orbit is:

$$p = eRB_R$$

where B_R in this case is the magnetic field at radius R. Clearly B_R must vary in time so that:

$$\frac{dp}{dt} = \frac{eRdB_R}{dt} = \frac{eR}{2}\frac{d\bar{B}}{dt}$$

that is B_R must increase so that it is always equal to $\frac{1}{2}\bar{B}$ if the electrons are to be confined to their orbit as they accelerate. This is the principle of the betatron, which can accelerate electrons up to energies of many MeV, when they begin to radiate significantly.

Faraday's disc

A homopolar generator can be made from a disc rotating in a steady magnetic field, as first shown by Faraday. In Fig. 5.7 the circular disc of radius a rotates at a steady angular velocity ω in a uniform field $\mathbf{B}$. The simplest type of disc is an insulating one with a conducting ring round its circumference, a conducting axle RO and a radial conducting wire OP embedded in it. The circuit QROPQ is then completed by the brushes on the moving parts at Q and R. Since there is a steady field the only source of e.m.f. must be a motional e.m.f. given by equation [5.6]:

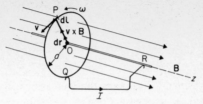

Fig. 5.7 Faraday's disc is a homopolar generator.

$$\mathcal{E} = \oint \mathbf{E}.\mathbf{dl} = \oint (\mathbf{v} \times \mathbf{B}).\mathbf{dl}.$$

The circuit QRO is stationary in the frame of **B** and so the only contributions to the e.m.f. come from OP and PQ. For OP, $\mathbf{v} \times \mathbf{B}$ is along **r** and $\mathbf{dl} = \mathbf{dr}$, while $v = r\omega$, so that

$$\oint (\mathbf{v} \times \mathbf{B}).\mathbf{dl} = \int_0^a r\omega B \mathrm{d}r = \frac{1}{2}a^2 \omega B.$$

And for PQ, $\mathbf{v} \times \mathbf{B}$ is normal to **dl** at all points so that the contribution to the integral is zero. Therefore $\mathcal{E} = \frac{1}{2}a^2 \omega B$ is the e.m.f. driving a current along the circuit in the direction QR.

In terms of Faraday's law (equation [5.4]), we must be careful to specify the flux being cut by the circuit. For the circuit in Fig. 5.7, the flux is cut as the radial wire OP sweeps round through angle POQ. If this angle is θ radians, then the flux cut $= B\pi a^2 (\theta/2\pi)$ and Faraday's law gives:

$$\mathcal{E} = -\frac{\mathrm{d}\Phi}{\mathrm{d}t} = -\frac{Ba^2}{2}\frac{\mathrm{d}\theta}{\mathrm{d}t} = -\frac{1}{2}a^2 \omega B$$

as before.

When the whole disc is a conductor (exercise 4), very high currents can be generated in the small resistance of the disc and so several brushes are joined together to conduct the radial currents back to the axle.

Mutual inductance

A typical example of a transformer e.m.f. (equation [5.8]) is provided by a coil 1 producing a time-varying magnetic field within the turns of a second coil 2 fixed to it (Fig. 5.8(a)). When the same **B** is parallel to the area S of each of N turns of a coil, the e.m.f. becomes:

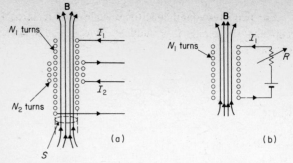

Fig. 5.8 (a) A mutual inductance. (b) A self-inductance.

$$\mathscr{E} = -\frac{d}{dt}(NBS)$$

that is, it is the negative of the rate of change of the flux linkage $N\Phi$.

Applying Ampère's law, $\oint \mathbf{B.ds} = \mu_0 I$, to each turn of coil 1 in Fig. 5.8(a), the field inside is:

$$B_1 = \mu_0 N_1 I_1/l$$

and for a long solenoid, B_0 outside is negligible. Therefore the flux linking coil 2 from coil 1 is:

$$N_2\Phi_{21} = N_2 B_1 S = \mu_0 N_1 N_2 S I_1/l$$

where I_1 is the only quantity varying with time. Hence the e.m.f. induced in coil 2 is:

$$\mathscr{E}_{21} = -\left(\frac{\mu_0 N_1 N_2 S}{l}\right)\frac{dI_1}{dt}.$$

Clearly $\mathscr{E}_{21}$ is proportional to dI_1/dt. The constant of proportionality, which depends only on the geometry of the coils, is called the *mutual inductance, M*. In particular M_{21} is the flux linking coil 2 due to *unit* current in coil 1, that is:

$$M_{21} = \frac{N_2\Phi_{21}}{I_1} \qquad\qquad [5.11]$$

and $\mathscr{E}_{21} = -M_{21}\frac{dI_1}{dt}.$

For two overwound coils there is clearly a reciprocal relationship and the e.m.f. $\mathscr{E}_{12}$ induced in coil 1 due to current I_2 varying is:

$$\mathscr{E}_{12} = -M_{12} \frac{dI_2}{dt} \qquad [5.12]$$

where

$$M_{12} = \frac{N_1 \Phi_{12}}{I_2}. \qquad [5.13]$$

For this case it is obvious that $M_{12} = M_{21} = M$, a result which can be proved for any pair of coupled circuits (Neumann's theorem).

Self-inductance

Faraday induction is not confined to pairs of circuits: we can have self-induction in a single coil. In Fig. 5.8(b) if we vary R then I_1 changes and so the flux Φ_{11} changes. This generates a self-e.m.f. given by:

$$\mathscr{E}_{11} = -\frac{d}{dt}(N_1 \Phi_{11}).$$

The *self-inductance* of a coil L is therefore the flux linkage in the coil per unit current in the coil, or

$$L = \frac{N_1 \Phi_{11}}{I_1} \qquad [5.14]$$

and

$$\mathscr{E} = -L \frac{dI_1}{dt}. \qquad [5.15]$$

The SI unit for both mutual and self-inductance is the *henry*, equivalent to 1 volt-second per ampere. Since $M_{21} = \mu_0 N_1 N_2 S/l$, we note that an alternative, and commonly used, unit for the magnetic constant μ_0 is henry per metre, so that:

$$\mu_0 = 4\pi \times 10^{-7} \, \text{H m}^{-1} \qquad [5.16]$$

an exact relationship. The self-inductance of a coil is

$$L = M_{11} = \mu_0 N^2 S/l \qquad [5.17]$$

and an inductance of 1 H requires a very large, air-cored solenoid (e.g. 7000 turns of diameter 0.1 m over a length 0.5 m). Commonly air-cored coils are in the range μH to mH and larger ones have cores of high permeability to enhance their value. At very high frequencies the 'skin effect' causes a small change in L, but for most purposes the self-inductance of an air-cored coil given by equation [5.15] is independent of frequency.

Coupled circuits

When two circuits are coupled, as in Fig. 5.9(a), the current in 1 depends on both the battery V_1 and the e.m.f. induced in it by variations in the current in 2. From equation [5.12],

$$\mathcal{E}_{12} = -M_{12} \frac{dI_2}{dt} = -M \frac{dI_2}{dt}$$

where the negative sign means that if both I_1 and I_2 are positive (anticlockwise) currents, then $\mathcal{E}_{12}$ will be opposed to V_1 when dI_2/dt is positive (increasing). If the polarity of V_1 is reversed, then I_1 is negative and so $\mathcal{E}_{12}$ and V_1 act in the same direction for increasing dI_2/dt.

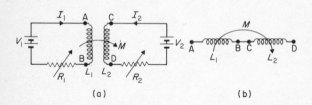

(a)   (b)

Fig. 5.9 (a) Coupled circuits. (b) Series coupled inductances.

The mutual inductance is reversed in sign if one of the coils is reversed, as can be seen more clearly in Fig. 5.9(b), where the total inductance will be:

$$L_{ABCD} = L_1 + L_2 + 2M \qquad [5.18]$$

or $\quad L_{ABCD} = L_1 + L_2 - 2M$

according to whether the currents in L_1 and L_2 are both of the same, or of opposite, signs. So, in general, the e.m.f. in circuit 1 of Fig. 5.9(a) is:

$$V_1 \pm M \frac{dI_2}{dt} - L_1 \frac{dI_1}{dt} = I_1 R$$

where the e.m.f. $\mathcal{E}_{11}$ from equation [5.15] has also been included.

When the coils L_1 and L_2 are coupled tightly together, for example by winding one on top of the other in a toroid, there is no leakage of magnetic flux and so:

$$\Phi_{12} = \Phi_{22} \quad \text{and} \quad \Phi_{21} = \Phi_{11}.$$

But $M_{12} = \dfrac{N_1 \Phi_{12}}{I} \quad \text{and} \quad M_{21} = \dfrac{N_2 \Phi_{21}}{I}.$

Therefore

$$M_{12} M_{21} = M^2 = N_1 N_2 \Phi_{22} \Phi_{11} / I_1 I_2$$

and, from equation [5.14] defining self-inductance,

$$M^2 = L_1 L_2$$

or $\quad M = \sqrt{L_1 L_2}.$ [5.19]

This is the maximum value of M for tight coupling. In general there is some flux leakage and

$$M = k \sqrt{L_1 L_2}$$ [5.20]

where $0 \leqslant k \leqslant 1$ and k is the coupling coefficient.

Magnetic energy

A coil with a current flowing in it stores magnetic energy, an outstanding example being a superconducting coil in its persistent mode. This energy is due to the rate of doing electrical work W by the induced e.m.f. $\mathcal{E}$ in the coil against the induced current I:

$$\frac{dW}{dt} = \mathcal{E}I = -LI\frac{dI}{dt}.$$

For a perfect (loss-less) coil, the total energy stored is therefore:

$$U = -W = \tfrac{1}{2} L I^2.$$ [5.21]

Chapter 6
Magnetism

In this chapter we extend magnetostatics to include matter in general, where previously we have considered the magnetic fields arising from electrons in a vacuum or free electrons in metals. We use Gauss's law for magnetic flux

$$\int_S \mathbf{B}.\mathbf{dS} = 0$$

Ampère's circulation law

$$\oint_C \mathbf{B}.\mathbf{ds} = \mu_0 \int_S \mathbf{j}.\mathbf{dS}$$

for steady currents and consider induced currents from Faraday's law

$$\oint_C \mathbf{E}.\mathbf{ds} = - \int_S \frac{\partial \mathbf{B}}{\partial t}.\mathbf{dS}.$$

All states of matter will be considered: gases, liquids and solids, especially special materials like iron. We first discuss the microscopic nature of magnetism, then define magnetisation **M**, the magnetising field **H** and find the boundary conditions for **B** and **H** between two media. We continue with an introduction to each of the commonest types of magnetism, dia-, para- and ferromagnetism, and conclude by discussing the production of both permanent and powerful magnetic fields.

6.1 Magnetisation of matter

The simplest model of an atom, the Bohr model (Fig. 6.1(a)) has at least one electron rotating in a fixed, circular orbit about the

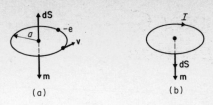

Fig. 6.1 (a) An orbiting electron in an atom is equivalent to (b) a magnetic dipole.

nucleus. If the orbit has area $dS = \pi a^2$ and the electron is orbiting at a speed v, its motion is equivalent to a current

$$I = -ev/2\pi a.$$

From a distance this orbiting electron is equivalent (Fig. 6.1(b)) to a magnetic dipole of moment

$$\mathbf{m} = I d\mathbf{S}. \tag{6.1}$$

Typical values of $a = 50\,\text{pm}$, $v = 10^6\,\text{m}\,\text{s}^{-1}$ show that m is about $10^{-23}\,\text{A}\,\text{m}^2$. Although this is a very small moment, significant magnetisation $\mathbf{M}$ of matter can result from the partial or complete alignment of many moments $\mathbf{m}$ in a volume V. The total magnetic moment is the vector sum of the individual moments and we define *magnetisation* as the total magnetic moment per unit volume,

$$\mathbf{M} = \Sigma \mathbf{m}/V. \tag{6.2}$$

The magnetic moments in matter arise not only from the orbital motion of electrons in atoms (atomic moments) but also from the intrinsic angular momentum (spin) of electrons (intrinsic moments) and from the spin of nucleons (nuclear moments). Magnetisation of matter by applied magnetic fields is a similar phenomenon to the polarisation of matter by applied electric fields. We found that the polarisation $\mathbf{P}$ of a dielectric was associated with an induced surface charge density, σ_p. We shall now show that the magnetisation $\mathbf{M}$ of matter is associated with an induced surface current density, i_m.

In Fig. 6.2(a) an elementary volume $dx\,dy\,dz$ of matter has been magnetised parallel to the applied field $\mathbf{B}$ (this is the case for

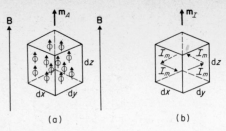

Fig. 6.2 (a) An elementary volume of magnetised matter is equivalent to (b) a surface magnetisation current, I_m.

a parallel or *paramagnetic material*, in contrast to an antiparallel or *diamagnetic* material). The atomic magnetic moments add vectorially to give a total moment m_A. This can be exactly equivalent to a single current loop (Fig. 6.2(b)) of current I_m around the volume element producing a magnetic moment:

$$m_I = I_m \, dx \, dy = m_A.$$

There the magnetisation of the elementary volume is of magnitude

$$M = \frac{m_A}{dx \, dy \, dz} = \frac{I_m}{dz}$$

and in the same direction as the applied field **B**. The term *surface current density* i_m is used for the surface current per unit length normal to the current, so that here:

$$M = \frac{I_m}{dz} = i_m \qquad [6.3]$$

which can be compared with $P = \sigma_p$.

In order to relate **M** to **B**, we first consider a larger volume (Fig. 6.3) of matter uniformly magnetised along $0z$. If this is divided into many elementary volumes $dx \, dy \, dz$, it is clear that the magnetisation currents I_m in each small cube will cancel at all the internal surfaces of adjacent cubes and also at all internal edges of the surfaces in the xy planes (see inset of the figure). There remain the surface currents at the other four faces in the xz and yz planes and these all act together to provide a surface current density $i_m = I_m/dz$, as before. Although we have proved

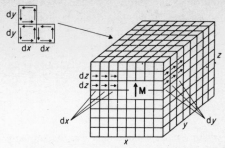

Fig. 6.3 A magnetised volume of matter is equivalent to a surface current density.

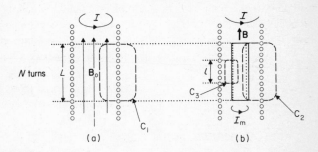

Fig. 6.4 Ampère's circulation law applied to: (a) empty solenoid with contour C_1; and (b) solenoid containing a paramagnetic with contour C_2. Contour C_3 is for the circulation of the magnetisation only.

this only for a cube, it is easy to see that i_m circulates around **M** as the current in a long solenoid circulates around **B** (Fig. 4.16 and 6.4(a)).

In the empty solenoid we have already seen that Ampère's law gives for the uniform, central field B_0:

$$\oint_{C_1} \mathbf{B.ds} = \mu_0 NI = B_0 L.$$

This can be expressed:

$$B_0 = \mu_0 (NI/L) = \mu_0 i_f \qquad [6.4]$$

where i_f is a *solenoidal current density* due to the free electrons in the conduction current I with units ampere-turns per metre.

When a paramagnetic rod is placed entirely in this central field, it is magnetised and its magnetisation M is equivalent to a uniform surface current density i_m. Clearly these surface currents increase the field in the solenoid, according to Ampère's law:

$$\oint_{C_2} \mathbf{B}.d\mathbf{s} = \mu_0(NI + i_m L) = BL$$

or $\quad B = \mu_0(i_f + i_m)$. $\hfill$ [6.5]

We have already shown that the magnetisation M is equal to i_m and, for a paramagnetic, is in the same direction as B. We now define the *magnetising field* H as that due to the solenoidal current density alone, so that $H = i_f$. For the empty solenoid, equation [6.4] can be rewritten:

$$\mathbf{B}_0 = \mu_0 \mathbf{H} \hfill [6.6]$$

and this is only true when there is no matter present. Thus H like D ignores the effects of introducing matter and is entirely due to the free, conduction electrons of magnetostatics. When matter is present, equation [6.5] can therefore be written:

$$\mathbf{B} = \mu_0(\mathbf{H} + \mathbf{M}). \hfill [6.7]$$

When the magnetic matter is linear, isotropic and homogeneous, M is proportional to H and we define the *magnetic suscepti-bility* χ_m as the dimensionless ratio M/H. This is the definition commonly accepted, but some authors have used $\chi_B = \mu_0 M/B$, which is also dimensionless. The *magnetic permeability* is defined as B/H, so that equation [6.7] can be written:

$$\mu = \frac{\mathbf{B}}{\mathbf{H}} = \mu_0(1 + \chi_m) \hfill [6.8]$$

or alternatively as

$$\mu = \frac{\mathbf{B}}{\mathbf{H}} = \frac{\mu_0}{(1 - \chi_B)}.$$

For paramagnetics in which $\chi_m \ll 1$ and positive, or diamagnetics in which $\chi_m \ll 1$ and negative, there is little difference between χ_B and χ_m. But in ferromagnetics where $\chi_m \gg 1$ and positive, M is only proportional to H for small ranges of H and χ_B is not the same as χ_m. The relative permeability $\mu_r = \mu/\mu_0$ is given by:

$$\mu_r = 1 + \chi_m. \hfill [6.9]$$

6.2 Characteristics of B and H

Circulation

We have seen that the circulation of **B**, given by Ampère's law

$$\oint_C \mathbf{B}.\mathbf{ds} = \mu_0 I$$

can be written in the presence of magnetised matter in a solenoid as:

$$\oint_C \mathbf{B}.\mathbf{ds} = \mu_0(I_f + I_m)$$

where I_f is the free, conduction current and I_m is the magnetisation current. Using equation [6.7] this becomes:

$$\oint_C \mathbf{H}.\mathbf{ds} + \oint_C \mathbf{M}.\mathbf{ds} = I_f + I_m.$$

From Fig. 6.4(b) the contour C_3 shows that the circulation of **M** is just I_m, since the contributions to **M.ds** are $i_m l$ within the paramagnetic, zero normal to **M** and zero outside the paramagnetic. Therefore, by subtraction, the circulation of **H** is:

$$\oint_C \mathbf{H}.\mathbf{ds} = I_f \qquad [6.10]$$

and this shows the importance of **H** as the magnetising field from conduction currents. However, it is only **B** that satisfies Gauss's law, $\int_S \mathbf{B}.\mathbf{dS} = 0$, and therefore only the lines of **B** are continuous with no sources or sinks (Fig. 6.5(a), (b)). At the surface of magnetised matter the lines of **M** disappear (Fig. 6.5(d)), while the corresponding lines of **H** begin there (Fig. 6.5(c)). This figure also shows how a magnetic medium of relative permeability μ_r increases **B** ($= \mu_r \mu_0 \mathbf{H}$), in contrast to a dielectric of relative permittivity ϵ_r which decreases **E** ($= \mathbf{D}/\epsilon_r \epsilon_0$).

Boundary conditions

How does the magnetic field change when it crosses the boundary between two magnetic media of permeabilities $\mu_1 = \mu_{r1}\mu_0$ and $\mu_2 = \mu_{r2}\mu_0$? To find out we apply Gauss's law for **B** and the

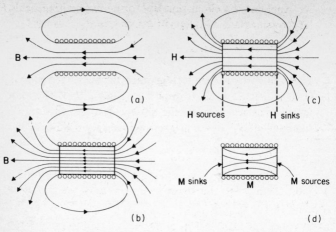

Fig. 6.5 Magnetic field **B** for (a) an empty solenoid and (b) a solenoid filled with a paramagnetic of relative permeability, μ_r, for which the magnetising field **H** lines are in (c) and the magnetisation **M** lines are in (d).

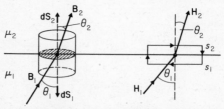

Fig. 6.6 Boundary conditions for the magnetic vectors **B** and **H** crossing between two magnetic media of permeabilities μ_1 and μ_2.

circulation law for **H** to the magnetic vectors shown in Fig. 6.6. Our treatment parallels that for **D** and **E**.

For the flux into and out of the Gaussian cylinder of cross-section dS and negligible height we have:

$$\mathbf{B}_1.d\mathbf{S}_1 + \mathbf{B}_2.d\mathbf{S}_2 = 0.$$

Hence only the normal component B_n of each magnetic field contributes and

$$B_{1n} = B_{2n}. \hspace{2cm} [6.11]$$

Applying the circulation law to the magnetising fields $\mathbf{H}_1$ and $\mathbf{H}_2$ crossing the closed loop of length s_1 and s_2, we have:

$$\int_C \mathbf{H}.\mathbf{ds} = \mathbf{H}_1.\mathbf{s}_1 + \mathbf{H}_2.\mathbf{s}_2 = 0$$

since there are no conduction currents present at the boundary of two magnetic media (except superconductors). The loop can be as near as we wish to the surface and so only the tangential component H_t of each magnetising field contributes and

$$H_{1t} = H_{2t}. \qquad [6.12]$$

At the boundary we therefore have continuity for B_n and H_t and when it is valid to write $\mathbf{B} = \mu_r \mu_0 \mathbf{H}$, we can write [6.11] and [6.12] as:

$$\mu_{r1} H_1 \cos \theta_1 = \mu_{r2} H_2 \cos \theta_2$$

$$H_1 \sin \theta_1 = H_2 \sin \theta_2.$$

We therefore get refraction of $\mathbf{B}$ and $\mathbf{H}$ at the boundary with the relation:

$$\frac{\tan \theta_1}{\tan \theta_2} = \frac{\mu_{r1}}{\mu_{r2}}. \qquad [6.13]$$

Energy density

For a coil of self-inductance L we showed that the energy stored in it (equation [5.21]), is

$$U = \tfrac{1}{2} L I^2$$

where, from equation [5.17], $L = \mu_0 N^2 S / l$. Applying these equations to the empty solenoid of Fig. 6.4 we have

$$B_0 = \mu_0 N I / l$$

and $\quad \mathbf{B}_0 = \mu_0 \mathbf{H}.$

Therefore

$$U = \frac{\mu_0}{2} \left(\frac{N^2 S I^2}{l} \right)$$

and the energy density

$$u = \frac{\mu_0}{2} \left(\frac{N^2 I^2}{l^2} \right) = \tfrac{1}{2} \mathbf{B_0.H}$$

since $\mathbf{B_0}$ and $\mathbf{H}$ are parallel inside a long solenoid.

For a filled solenoid, if the magnetic material is linear, isotropic and homogeneous then $\mathbf{B} = \mu\mathbf{H}$ (equation [6.8]), and the inductance increases to $L = \mu N^2 S/l$. Therefore the energy density is

$$u = \frac{\mu}{2} \left(\frac{N^2 I^2}{l^2} \right) = \tfrac{1}{2} \mathbf{B.H}. \tag{6.14}$$

We showed in section 2.4 that electrostatic energy is stored in the electric field and a similar argument can be used to show that magnetic energy is stored in the magnetic field. Therefore, we can write for the total magnetic energy

$$U = \tfrac{1}{2} \int_\tau \mathbf{B.H} d\tau \tag{6.15}$$

which is the corresponding equation to [2.36] for electric energy.

6.3 Magnetism in matter

For most substances magnetic effects are very small and can only be seen using high magnetic fields or sensitive detectors like those involved in nuclear magnetic resonance methods. In these substances the relative permeability $\mu_r \ll 1$, but in ferromagnetics such as iron, cobalt and nickel, $\mu_r \gg 1$ and is found from $dB/(\mu_0 dH)$, as $\mathbf{B}$ is not proportional to $\mathbf{H}$. Here we consider first diamagnetics, in which the induced magnetism acquires a dipole moment opposed to the applied field, and then paramagnetism where permanent dipole moments are aligned parallel to the applied field. In each we consider only the orbital motion of electrons in atoms, although most atomic magnetism arises from the intrinsic moments of the electrons associated with their spin. However, the principles of dia- and paramagnetism can be understood in terms of the orbital moments.

Diamagnetics

An atomic dipole arises from an orbiting electron on Bohr theory (Figs. 6.1 and 6.7) and has a moment, from equation [6.1],

$$\mathbf{m} = I d\mathbf{S} = \frac{-ev}{2\pi r} (\pi r^2) \hat{\mathbf{n}} = \frac{-evr}{2} \hat{\mathbf{n}} \qquad [6.16]$$

where $\hat{\mathbf{n}}$ is the normal for the electron orbit in Fig. 6.7(b). When a

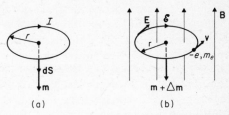

(a)   (b)

Fig. 6.7 (a) An atomic dipole of moment **m**. (b) Enhanced to **m** + Δ**m** by the applied field **B**.

uniform magnetic field is applied to this electron it induces an e.m.f. $\mathcal{E}$ in the 'circuit' given by Faraday's law (equation [5.8])

$$\mathcal{E} = \oint_C \mathbf{E}.d\mathbf{s} = -\int_S \frac{\partial \mathbf{B}}{\partial t}.d\mathbf{S}$$

which becomes

$$2\pi r E = -\frac{dB}{dt} (\pi r^2).$$

By Newton's second law, the electron of mass m_e is accelerated by the force $-e\mathbf{E}$ acting on it:

$$m_e \frac{dv}{dt} = -eE = \frac{er}{2} \frac{dB}{dt}.$$

Integrating this over the time the field increases from 0 to B and the speed v increases by Δv, where:

$$\Delta v = \left(\frac{er}{2m_e}\right) B \qquad [6.17]$$

producing an incremental moment from the equation [6.16] of

$$\Delta m = \frac{er}{2} \Delta v = \frac{e^2 r^2}{4m_e} B$$

which by Lenz's law opposes **B** so that

$$\Delta\mathbf{m} = \frac{-e^2 r^2}{4m_e}\,\mathbf{B}. \qquad [6.18]$$

The value of the orbital radius r results from a balance between the Coulomb attraction **F** of the nucleus for the electron and the centrifugal force $m_e v^2/r$. The Lorentz force due to **B** on the electron is $-e\mathbf{v} \times \mathbf{B}$ and this acts to increase **F** by evB. On the other hand, the increased speed Δv produces an increase $2m_e v\Delta v/r$ in the centrifugal force and this, from equation [6.17], exactly balances the increase in **F**. Therefore the effect of **B** is to produce a smaller moment $(\mathbf{m} + \Delta\mathbf{m})$, where $\Delta\mathbf{m}$ (negative) is given by equation [6.18], but to maintain the electron in its original orbit.

The magnetisation of a diamagnetic containing N atoms per unit volume, each with Z orbiting electrons on radii with a mean square radius $\langle r^2 \rangle$ is therefore:

$$\mathbf{M} = N\Delta\mathbf{m} = \left(\frac{-e^2 NZ\langle r^2\rangle}{4m_e}\right)\mathbf{B}$$

and the corresponding susceptibility is

$$\chi_B = \frac{\mu_0 M}{B} = -\frac{\mu_0 e^2 N}{4m_e}\,Z\langle r^2\rangle \triangleq \chi_m \qquad [6.19]$$

One possible model for such a diamagnetic is that its atomic electrons are paired off with opposite rotations and so opposing dipole moments (Fig. 6.8(a)). Application of a magnetic field **B** then slows down the electron in orbit 1 and accelerates that in

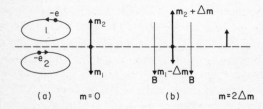

Fig. 6.8 A diamagnetic could consist of an electron pair with opposing dipole moments. (a) $B = 0$. (b) **B** produces a moment $2\Delta m$.

orbit 2 with the net result that they acquire a moment $2\Delta \mathbf{m}$ opposing $\mathbf{B}$ (Fig. 6.8(b)). In terms of the angular velocity $\omega = v/r$ of each electron, the change in angular velocity is called the *Larmor (angular) frequency* ω_L, which, from equation [6.17], is:

$$\omega_L = eB/2m_e. \qquad [6.20]$$

The angular velocity of orbit 1 thus becomes $(\omega_0 + \omega_L)$ and that of orbit 2, $(\omega_0 - \omega_L)$.

This model of a diamagnetic implies that χ_m is independent of temperature, since the core structure of an atom is normally unchanged by thermal vibrations. For a mole of solid diamagnetic occupying 10 cm³, $N = 6 \times 10^{28}$ m⁻³ and if we put $Z = 29$, $\langle r^2 \rangle = a_0$, equation [6.19] predicts χ_m of about -40×10^{-6}, which is a similar order of magnitude to χ_m measured for copper (-10×10^{-6}) and glass (-110×10^{-6}). Similarly for a gas at STP with $N = 6 \times 10^{25}$ m⁻³, χ_m is about -40×10^{-9}, which is not very different from χ_m for nitrogen gas (-5×10^{-9}).

Paramagnetics

In paramagnetics each atom has a small permanent dipole moment $\mathbf{m}$ due to its orbiting electrons (and their spin). On Bohr theory each electron with $m = \frac{1}{2}evr$ (equation [6.16]) has angular momentum $m_e vr = n\hbar$, where n is the number of the orbit and so:

$$m = n(e\hbar/2m_e). \qquad [6.21]$$

The moment of an electron in the first Bohr orbit is called the *Bohr magneton* m_B and is a unit of about 9×10^{-24} A m². When the moments of the core electrons in a paramagnetic atom or molecule have been added vectorially, the total moment should be of the order of 10^{-23} A m², if other effects are not present.

How many of these dipoles are likely to be aligned when we apply a magnetic field? If we do the experiment at room temperature the thermal energy of about $kT = 1.4 \times 10^{-23} \times 300$ joules, roughly 25 meV, will tend to keep them pointing in random directions. We saw in Chapter 4 that there is a torque $\mathbf{m} \times \mathbf{B}$ (equation [4.13]) tending to align a magnetic dipole with an applied field. An unaligned dipole therefore has a greater potential energy than an aligned one. If we take the zero of potential energy, which is arbitrary, as that when **m** is normal to **B**, then the energy lost by the dipole during alignment is **m.B**. Therefore the potential energy of the dipole in the field is:

$$U = -\mathbf{m}.\mathbf{B} \qquad [6.22]$$

and the maximum energy that could be given to a dipole would be to completely reverse its polarity from $-\mathbf{m}$ to $+\mathbf{m} = 2mB$. If m is about $10^{-23}\,\mathrm{A\,m^2}$ and a large field, say 5 T, is applied, U will not exceed 10^{-22} joules or roughly 1 meV.

Thus only a small fraction f of the dipoles will be aligned parallel to **B** and it can be shown, from statistical mechanics, that this fraction is:

$$f = \frac{mB}{3kT}. \qquad [6.23]$$

Therefore the magnetisation of a paramagnetic with N atoms per unit volume is, from equation [6.2],

$$\mathbf{M} = \frac{\Sigma \mathbf{m}}{V} = N\mathbf{m}f$$

or $\quad \mathbf{M} = \left(\frac{Nm^2}{3\,kT}\right)\mathbf{B}$

and $\quad \chi_m = \frac{M}{H} = \frac{\mu_0 Nm^2}{3\,kT}. \qquad [6.24]$

This is known as *Curie's law* and shows that χ_m increases as $1/T$ at low temperatures, in contrast to the diamagnetics, where χ_m in equation [6.19] is independent of temperature.

Some paramagnetic salts, such as chromium potassium alum, can be magnetically saturated at low temperatures with a super-conducting solenoid providing, say, 2 T at 1 K. Others, such as cerium magnesium nitrate, continue to obey Curie's law to very low (millikelvin) temperatures and so their reciprocal suscepti-bility as a function of temperature provides an excellent thermometer. These are in direct contrast to electric dipole moments, which usually cannot be saturated at low temperatures, since they rely on the displacement of electron distributions (in atoms) or their rotation (in molecules), movements that would be frozen in most solids.

In metals the major contribution is the Pauli spin paramagnetism of the conduction electrons, in which at a temperature T only the small fraction T/T_F, where T_F is the Fermi temperature of about 10^5 K, take part. This is discussed in texts on the solid state.

In gases the total susceptibility on the Bohr model presented here would be:

$$\chi_m = N\mu_0 \left(\frac{m^2}{3kT} - \frac{e^2 Z\langle r^2 \rangle}{4m_e} \right) \qquad [6.25]$$

and experiments over a range of temperatures enable both m and $\langle r^2 \rangle$ to be measured. The moments found are of the order of a Bohr magneton in a paramagnetic gas like oxygen and in the diamagnetic inert gases the radii of the atoms are about one Bohr radius (5×10^{-11} m), so that Bohr's theory does give reasonable values for the static magnetic susceptibility of gases.

Ferromagnetics

Ferromagnetics are materials in which magnetisation occurs spontaneously, that is without the application of an external magnetic field. The commonest ferromagnetic is iron and its alloys (steels), but it is well known that an iron rod is not a good magnet. There are two reasons for this, shown in Figs. 6.9 and 6.10. First, the material divides up into regions which are perfect magnets, known as *domains*, but these domains are magnetised in many different directions. In Fig. 6.9 a ferromagnetic which consisted of only one domain is compared with one having four domains, magnetised alternately in opposite directions. The single domain has a large external magnetic field, which is energetically less favourable than the multi-domain sample with a negligible external field. The size of the domains in practice is a balance between the energy saved through their existence and the energy used in creating the boundaries between them.

The second reason is the existence of many differently orientated small crystals, known as *grains*, in ordinary, polycrystalline

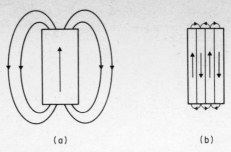

Fig. 6.9 (a) A single domain and (b) four domains in a single crystal of a ferromagnetic.

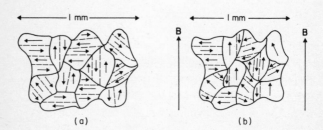

Fig. 6.10 A ferromagnetic: (a) in its unmagnetised state; (b) in a magnetic field.

iron. The net result is that spontaneously magnetised iron at room temperature has, under a microscope with a suitable coating, the appearance of Fig. 6.10(a). Each grain consists of several domains, magnetised in a direction corresponding to the crystallographic orientations of the grains. When a magnetic field is applied (Fig. 6.10(b)) the initial effect is for the domains that are favourably orientated to grow in size at the expense of their less fortunate neighbours. Such an effect is reversible when the field is removed and corresponds to the initial magnetising region, OA in Fig. 6.11(a). A larger magnetic field will start to rotate the domains within the grains, producing greater magnetisation, as AB in Fig. 6.11(a). Finally, at sufficiently high fields the magnetisation saturates, when all the domains are aligned along the applied field, as at C in Fig. 6.11(a).

Experimentally a *B–H* curve of this type can be obtained by

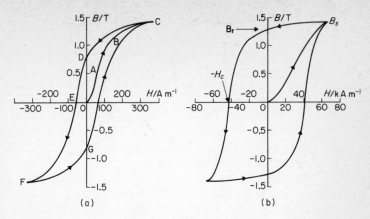

Fig. 6.11 Hysteresis curves for: (a) polycrystalline iron; (b) a permanent magnet alloy.

winding a toroidal coil (Fig. 4.15) around an iron ring, when the magnetising field is given by $H = NI/l$, where the toroid has N turns over a length l and carries a current I (equations [6.4] and [6.6]), while B is measured by induction in a second coil attached to a fluxmeter. Following initial magnetisation to saturation, when the current I and so field H are reduced to zero, there is a *remanence* (OD in Fig. 6.11(a)) and for complete demagnetisation it is necessary to apply a reversed field OE, known as the *coercivity*. As the field continues to be reversed the magnetisation eventually saturates in the opposite direction at F and the cycle is completed by FGC. The complete curve is a *hysteresis loop* and represents a significant loss of energy through its irreversibility.

The loss occurs in the movements of the domain boundaries and comes from the source of the current in the coil. By Faraday's law an e.m.f. $\mathcal{E}$ is induced in the winding as B changes given by:

$$\mathcal{E} = -NS \frac{dB}{dt}$$

where S is the cross-sectional area of the iron ring. This e.m.f. will oppose the increase in the current and so the extra power from the source to maintain the current will be:

$$\frac{dU}{dt} = -I\mathcal{E} = INS\frac{dB}{dt} = HSl\frac{dB}{dt}.$$

The volume of the ring is Sl and so the energy density in a complete hysteresis loop will be:

$$u = \oint H dB \qquad\qquad [6.26]$$

where the integral is just the area of the loop on the B–H plot.

Materials such as soft (pure) iron have comparatively small hysteresis loops (Fig. 6.11(a)) and so are used for alternating currents in chokes and transformers, while specially selected iron alloys (steels) can have very large loops (Fig. 6.11(b)). Here the saturation field B_s is similar to that for iron, but the magnetising and demagnetising fields are very much larger (note the change of scale in H from $A\,m^{-1}$ to $kA\,m^{-1}$). The result is that the area of the loop and the coercivity $(-H_c)$ are much larger and so these alloys make excellent permanent magnets. Typically the energy density in a hysteresis loop ranges from about $100\,J\,m^{-3}$ in a soft ferromagnetic to about $10^5\,J\,m^{-3}$ in a very hard one.

When ferromagnetis are heated above their *Curie point*, T_c, they become paramagnetics obeying a Curie–Weiss law,

$$\chi_m = \frac{C}{T - T_c} \qquad\qquad [6.27]$$

which differs from Curie's law (equation [6.24]). At the Curie point the interactions between the electron spins undergo a cooperative transition, known as an order–disorder transition, which results in the spontaneous magnetisation and the formation of the domains. In Fig. 6.12 the resulting magnetisation is seen to increase sharply just below T_c and then to saturate at low temperatures. It is only in recent years that theories in quantum statistics have been devised to explain such very strong interactions.

A special class of *ferrimagnetics* are ferromagnetic insulators, such as ferrites (oxides of iron), which have almost rectangular hysteresis loops and so can be switched rapidly from $-B_s$ to $+B_s$. This makes them particularly suitable for the cores of high frequency transformers, for magnetic tapes and for computer memories. In a few materials called *antiferromagnetics*, such as

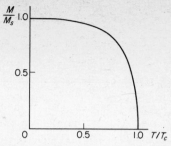

Fig. 6.12 Spontaneous magnetisation of a ferromagnetic when cooled below its Curie point, T_c.

chromium, magnetic interactions between the atomic spins cause the spins to be alternatively pointing in opposite directions and so the net magnetisation is quite small. However they do exhibit spontaneous magnetisation below a temperature called the *Néel point* and show similar nonlinear behaviour to ferromagnetics.

6.4 Production of magnetic fields

There are three basic arrangements for producing strong magnetic fields: solenoids, electromagnets and permanent magnets. We consider each of these in turn and apply the following equations to solve the magnetic circuits involved:

Gauss's law

$$\int_S \mathbf{B.dS} = 0 \qquad\qquad [4.28]$$

Circulation law for **H**

$$\oint_C \mathbf{H.ds} = I_f. \qquad\qquad [6.10]$$

For magnetic media

$$\mathbf{B} = \mu_r \mu_0 \mathbf{H} \qquad\qquad [6.8]$$

can be applied at a point on the hysteresis loop as

$$\mu_r = dB/(\mu_0 dH).$$

Solenoids

These rely on a high current to provide an axial field $\mu_0 NI/l$ (Fig. 6.4(a)). The highest steady fields are provided by Bitter solenoids formed from stacks of water-cooled, perforated copper discs having up to 1000 A at 200 V from powerful generators passing through them. For a bore of 3–4 cm fields of 25–20 T are available in several countries, but such installations are extremely expensive to build and operate. For most purposes super-conducting solenoids, using fine wires of niobium–titanium (Nb–Ti) or niobium–tin ($Nb_3 Sn$) embedded in a copper matrix, are used to produce fields in the range 1–15 T from laboratory sizes to large installations for the confinement of plasmas or hydrogen bubble chambers. They operate in liquid helium at 4.2 K, but once the currents have been established in them they persist indefinitely with negligible electrical power loss. Laboratory magnets can have room temperature axial holes, for example, for optical or magnetic resonance experiments.

Still higher fields are possible as short pulses due to extremely high discharge currents from banks of low-loss capacitors into small, rigid, single turn coils. Transient fields of 100 T or more have been used for example in magneto-optical spectroscopy. The highest transient fields have been produced by flux compression in magnetic implosions for about a microsecond.

Electromagnets

A laboratory electromagnet consists of an insulated copper coil around a ferromagnetic core to concentrate the flux in a small air-gap and so provide a strong field at room temperature for susceptibility measurements or resonance experiments. It can be analysed as a torus with a core (Fig. 6.13(a)). If we assume negligible' flux leakage, equations [6.10] and [6.8] become:

$$\sum \frac{B_i l_i}{\mu_r \mu_0} = NI \qquad [6.28]$$

where i refers to either the core (m) or the gap (g). The flux Φ is continuous (Fig. 6.13(b)) and so we can write, by analogy with Ohm's law,

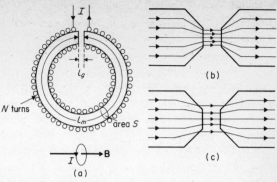

Fig. 6.13 (a) An electromagnet with air gap. (b) Magnetic circuit at the air gap. (c) Flux leakage at the air gap.

$$NI = \Phi \sum \frac{l_i}{\mu_r \mu_0 S_i} = \Phi \Sigma \mathscr{R} \qquad [6.29]$$

where NI is the *magnetomotive force* $\mathscr{F}$ and $\mathscr{R}$ is the magnetic *reluctance* of the circuit. From this equation it follows that reluctances add in series and parallel like resistors and so it does have an application in more complex magnetic circuits. However it ignores the small flux leakage that occurs in practice and is exaggerated in Fig. 6.13(c).

From Fig. 6.13(a) we have:

$$\mathscr{R} = \frac{l_m}{\mu_r \mu_0 S} + \frac{l_g}{\mu_0 S} \qquad [6.30]$$

and we see that most of the reluctance is in the air gap, since μ_r for a typical core is several thousand. Using equation [6.29], the flux is:

$$\Phi = \frac{\mu_0 NIS}{\left(\dfrac{l_m}{\mu_r} + l_g\right)}$$

and for plane pole pieces

$$B_m = B_g = \frac{\mu_0 NI}{\left(\dfrac{l_m}{\mu_r} + l_g\right)}.$$

On the other hand the magnetising fields are:

$$H_g = \frac{NI}{\left(\dfrac{l_m}{\mu_r} + l_g\right)} \quad \text{and} \quad H_m = \frac{NI}{(l_m + \mu_r l_g)}$$

so that the gap in the ring:

1. reduces B drastically; and
2. concentrates H in the gap ($H_g \gg H_m$).

Weiss electromagnets (Fig. 6.14) have large, steerable yokes and are often mounted on rails so that they can be used in more

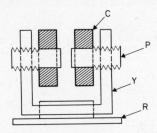

Fig. 6.14 A Weiss electromagnet with coils C mounted on adjustable pole pieces P and a yoke Y on a rotating base R.

than one experiment. The coils are watercooled, wound on adjustable, soft-iron pole pieces (to give a variable gap) and mounted on a steel yoke. They are normally supplied from stabilised power supplies to give either a uniform field (with flat pole pieces up to 300 mm diameter) or a concentrated field (with tapered pole pieces). The largest Weiss magnet ever built produced about 7 T from 100 kW and weighed 35 tonnes.

Permanent magnets

Permanent magnets are limited by the remanence B_r of known alloys to about 1 T (Fig. 6.15), but are compact, cheap and portable. They are commonly used with magnetrons in radar, for the non-destructive testing of materials and as standards for calibrating magnetometers.

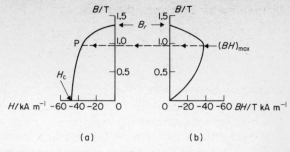

Fig. 6.15 (a) Demagnetisation curve for a permanent magnet alloy, (b) *BH* curve to find optimum size for a permanent magnet.

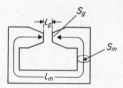

Fig. 6.16 A permanent magnet.

Applying equation [6.10] to the magnetic circuit in the permanent magnet of Fig. 6.16,

$$\oint_C \mathbf{H.ds} = H_g l_g + H_m l_m = 0 \qquad [6.31]$$

since there are no conduction currents. Thus H_g and H_m are in opposite directions, so that H_m is the *demagnetising field* of the magnet. For negligible flux leakage,

$$\Phi = B_g S_g = B_m S_m. \qquad [6.32]$$

Multiplying equations [6.31] and [6.32]

$$B_g H_g l_g S_g = -B_m H_m l_m S_m.$$

It is of interest to compare the magnetisation of a permanent bar magnet (Fig. 6.17) with that of a paramagnetic material (Fig. 6.5). In both cases the lines of **B** are continuous and show how **B** is enhanced in the material. On the other hand the magnetising field **H** in Fig. 6.5(c) is replaced by the demagnetising field $\mathbf{H}_m$ in Fig. 6.17(b).

A permanent magnet designed to produce a certain field B_g

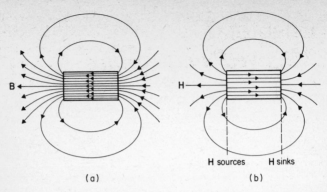

Fig. 6.17 (a) Magnetic field **B** for a permanent bar magnet. (b) Magnetising field **H** outside and demagnetising field H_m inside a permanent magnet.

($= \mu_0 H_g$) in a gap of length l_g and cross-section S_g will be of minimum size and cost if it is operated with $(B_m H_m)$ at its maximum value and so minimum volume $l_m S_m$ of the yoke. In Fig. 6.15(b) the product BH is plotted against B for the ferromagnetic alloy whose demagnetisation curve is given in Fig. 6.15(a). It is evident that the optimum BH value occurs at point P and that the best material for a high-field permanent magnet is one with both a large remanence B_r and large coercivity H_c. To preserve the magnetisation it is usual to place a 'keeper' of soft iron in the gap when the magnet is not in use. Since soft iron has a high permeability, equation [6.31] shows that it reduces the demagnetising field H_m almost to zero.

The magnetic energy density in the gap is, by equation [6.14]

$$u = \tfrac{1}{2} \frac{B_g^{\,2}}{\mu_0}.$$

By the principle of virtual work, the attractive force per unit area between the pole faces of a permanent magnet is just:

$$\frac{F}{S_g} = \tfrac{1}{2} \frac{B_g^{\,2}}{\mu_0}.$$

The construction of a permanent magnet must therefore be rigid enough to keep the air gap constant and resist this magnetic stress.

Chapter 7
Maxwell's equations

In this chapter we collect together the basic equations of electro-magnetism and express them in the form first devised by Maxwell to represent correctly the relationships between the electric field **E** and the magnetic field **B** in the presence of electric charges and electric currents, whether steady or rapidly fluctuating, in a vacuum or in matter. These are *Maxwell's equations.*

We shall find that we have already discussed three of these equations, due to Gauss and Faraday, but that Ampère's law has to be modified to allow for varying electric fields, whence it becomes known as Maxwell's law. We conclude with comments on the differences between statics and dynamics in electro-magnetism and the solutions that are developed in texts on electromagnetic theory.

7.1 Gauss's and Faraday's laws

Maxwell's equations express the fluxes and circulations of the electric and magnetic field vectors in differential form. The first one is derived from Gauss's law for the electric field,

$$\int_S \mathbf{E.dS} = \frac{1}{\epsilon_0} \int_V \rho d\tau \qquad [2.9]$$

which with Gauss's divergence theorem became:

$$\boxed{\text{div } \mathbf{E} = \rho/\epsilon_0.} \qquad [3.3]$$

The second, also due to Gauss, was for the flux of the magnetic field,

$$\int_S \mathbf{B}.\mathbf{dS} = 0 \qquad\qquad [4.28]$$

which in differential form is:

$$\boxed{\operatorname{div} \mathbf{B} = 0.} \qquad\qquad [4.29]$$

The third equation is derived from Faraday's law of electromagnetic induction:

$$\oint_C \mathbf{E}.\mathbf{ds} = - \int_S \frac{\partial \mathbf{B}}{\partial t}.\mathbf{dS} \qquad\qquad [5.8]$$

which with Stokes's theorem (equation [3.6]) led to:

$$\boxed{\operatorname{curl} \mathbf{E} = -\frac{\partial \mathbf{B}}{\partial t}.} \qquad\qquad [5.9]$$

These equations are true for all electromagnetic fields, for moving charges as well as stationary charges, for high frequencies as well as steady states, although it is necessary to consider relativistic effects to prove this statement.

7.2 Ampère's and Maxwell's laws

It would be logical at this point to expect that the fourth Maxwell equation would be derived from Ampère's law:

$$\oint_C \mathbf{B}.\mathbf{ds} = \mu_0 \int_S \mathbf{j}.\mathbf{dS} \qquad\qquad [4.24]$$

which correctly represents the circulation of the magnetic field for steady currents as μ_0 times the current density flux enclosed. But Maxwell noticed that when he applied this equation to the charging of a capacitor it did not work: the circulation around a contour C depended on where the imaginary surface S was drawn (Fig. 7.1). For the plane surface S_1, which cuts the current I, equation [4.24] gives:

$$\oint_C \mathbf{B}.\mathbf{ds} = \mu_0 I$$

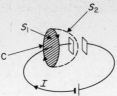

Fig. 7.1 A displacement current must exist in the capacitor.

but a second surface S_2 for the same contour C does not cut the current and so for this surface:

$$\oint_C \mathbf{B.ds} = 0 \,!$$

Maxwell argued that there must be a *displacement current* in the space between the capacitor plates which was equivalent to the external current. In a parallel plate capacitor the electric field $E = \sigma/\epsilon_0$ (equation [2.18]) and so if the plates are of area A,

$$E = \frac{Q}{\epsilon_0 A}$$

where Q is the charge on the plates. As the capacitor is charged the charging current is:

$$I = \frac{\partial Q}{\partial t} = \epsilon_0 A \frac{\partial E}{\partial t}.$$

Maxwell therefore modified Ampère's law by adding the flux of this displacement current giving:

$$\oint_C \mathbf{B.ds} = \mu_0 \left(I + \epsilon_0 A \frac{\partial E}{\partial t} \right).$$

Then for surface S_1 the circulation is $\mu_0 I$ and for surface S_2 it is

$$\mu_0 \epsilon_0 A \frac{\partial E}{\partial t} = \mu_0 I$$

and so constant. In general, therefore,

$$\oint_C \mathbf{B.ds} = \mu_0 \left\{ \int_S \mathbf{j.dS} + \int_S \epsilon_0 \frac{\partial E}{\partial t} \mathbf{.dS} \right\} \qquad [7.1]$$

is the integral form of Maxwell's law, which, with Stokes's theorem, becomes the fourth Maxwell equation:

$$\text{curl } \mathbf{B} = \mu_0 \left(\mathbf{j} + \epsilon_0 \frac{\partial \mathbf{E}}{\partial t} \right). \qquad [7.2]$$

All electromagnetic fields satisfy these four Maxwell equations and with the electromagnetic force law:

$$\mathbf{F} = q\mathbf{E} + q\mathbf{v} \times \mathbf{B} \qquad [4.9]$$

they summarise the whole of electromagnetism.

7.3 Statics and dynamics

We began electromagnetism by stating Coulomb's law and developing electrostatics. How many of our earlier equations are true for electrodynamics? Well, Coulomb's law obviously is not, for as soon as the charges move there is an electromagnetic force on them and we must use equation [4.9]. Then the concept of the electric field as the gradient of a scalar potential:

$$\mathbf{E} = -\text{grad } \phi \qquad [2.17]$$

is only true for static fields, since it is based on the circulation law

$$\oint_C \mathbf{E}.\mathbf{ds} = 0 \qquad [2.10]$$

which we saw in Chapter 5 became Faraday's law of electromagnetic induction:

$$\oint_C \mathbf{E}.\mathbf{ds} = - \int_S \frac{\partial \mathbf{B}}{\partial t}.\mathbf{dS} \qquad [5.8]$$

the integral form of Maxwell's third equation.

It follows that Laplace's and Poisson's equations for $\nabla^2 \phi$ are only valid for electrostatic fields and have to be modified in electrodynamics. On the other hand, the expressions that we have derived in electrostatics and in magnetism for electric and magnetic energy are true functions of the electromagnetic field at all frequencies. That is, the energy of an electromagnetic field is:

$$U = \tfrac{1}{2} \int_{\tau} \mathbf{D.E} \, d\tau \qquad [2.36]$$

plus $U = \tfrac{1}{2} \int_{\tau} \mathbf{B.H} \, d\tau.$ $\qquad [6.15]$

Of course such a statement has to be justified and is in texts on electromagnetic theory.

Finally, as Maxwell showed, the beautiful picture of a conductor as an equipotential surface with no electric field inside it is only true for electrostatics. In a conductor electrodynamic fields produce currents and so cause Ohmic losses. The simple pictures of capacitors having only a capacitance C and of inductors having only an inductance L break down at high frequencies, even if the inductor is wound with superconducting wire and an excellent dielectric like mica is used in the capacitor.

7.4 Solutions

We have presented the four Maxwell equations in terms of the electric and magnetic fields, **E** and **B** only. Many physicists prefer to use all four vectors **E**, **D**, **B** and **H** with the definitions $\mathbf{D} = \epsilon_0 \mathbf{E} + \mathbf{P}$ and $\mathbf{B} = \mu_0(\mathbf{H} + \mathbf{M})$ understood. Then Maxwell's equations become:

$$\text{div } \mathbf{D} = \rho_f \qquad [3.4]$$

$$\text{div } \mathbf{B} = 0 \qquad [4.29]$$

$$\text{curl } \mathbf{E} = -\frac{\partial \mathbf{B}}{\partial t} \qquad [5.9]$$

and $\text{curl } \mathbf{H} = \mathbf{j}_f + \dfrac{\partial \mathbf{D}}{\partial t}$ $\qquad [7.3]$

The last equation follows when Maxwell's law is applied to matter. We have already shown that the circulation of **H** is

$$\oint_C \mathbf{H.ds} = I_f \qquad [6.10]$$

which with

$$I_f = \int_S \mathbf{j}_f . \mathbf{dS}$$

and Stokes's theorem becomes:

$$\text{curl } \mathbf{H} = \mathbf{j}_f.$$

If the material is a dielectric there may be in addition a polarisation current

$$\mathbf{j}_p = \frac{\partial \mathbf{P}}{\partial t}$$

and when this is added to the displacement current $\epsilon_0 \partial \mathbf{E}/\partial t$ in a vacuum it becomes $\partial \mathbf{D}/\partial t$. Therefore, the fourth Maxwell equation can be written either as [7.2] or [7.3] and both sets of equations apply to nonlinear, anisotropic, non-homogeneous media.

An important principle in electromagnetism is the conservation of electric charge. It is recognised as of similar validity to the principles of conservation of energy and of momentum throughout physics. In integral form we had:

$$\int_S \mathbf{j}.\mathbf{dS} = \int \frac{\mathrm{d}q}{\mathrm{d}t} \tag{4.2}$$

where the charge q is flowing out of a surface of area S. If S is a closed surface and the charge density inside is ρ, then [4.2] can be written:

$$\int_S \mathbf{j}.\mathbf{dS} = -\frac{\mathrm{d}}{\mathrm{d}t} \left(\int_V \rho \, \mathrm{d}\tau \right). \tag{7.4}$$

By applying Gauss's divergence theorem (equation [3.2]) this becomes:

$$\int_S \mathbf{j}.\mathbf{dS} = \int_V \text{div } \mathbf{j} \, \mathrm{d}\tau. \tag{7.5}$$

If we apply equations [7.4] and [7.5] to a small volume $\mathrm{d}\tau$, then we obtain the *equation of continuity*:

$$\boxed{\text{div } \mathbf{j} = -\frac{\partial \rho}{\partial t}.} \tag{7.6}$$

This equation is not, however, additional to Maxwell's equations, because it is inherent in them.

The simplest way of showing that Maxwell's equations contain the principle of conservation of charge is by combining the equations:

$$\text{div } \mathbf{D} = \rho_f \qquad\qquad\qquad [3.4]$$

and $\quad \text{curl } \mathbf{H} = \mathbf{j}_f + \dfrac{\partial \mathbf{D}}{\partial t}. \qquad\qquad\qquad [7.3]$

From [7.3]

$$\text{div curl } \mathbf{H} = \text{div } \mathbf{j}_f + \text{div } \frac{\partial \mathbf{D}}{\partial t} = 0$$

since the divergence of a curl of any vector is identically zero. Therefore

$$\text{div } \mathbf{j}_f = -\text{div}\left(\frac{\partial \mathbf{D}}{\partial t}\right) = -\frac{\partial \rho_f}{\partial t}$$

from [3.4] and we recover equation [7.6] for the free charge density ρ_f and the conduction current density $\mathbf{j}_f$. In a similar way it can be shown that equation [7.2], where $\mathbf{j}$ is the current density in matter and can include a polarisation current density $\partial \mathbf{P}/\partial t$ and a magnetisation current density curl $\mathbf{M}$, leads to equation [7.6] for the total charge density

$$\rho = \rho_f + \rho_p.$$

To solve Maxwell's equations for $\mathbf{E}$ and $\mathbf{B}$ we have to integrate them for the proper boundary conditions. This is simplest in free space, but solutions can be found for dielectrics, semiconductors, conductors and indeed for any crystalline or amorphous material. The solutions include the simplest examples with high symmetry that we have discussed for distributions of static charges and steady currents. However, it was Maxwell's deduction that electromagnetic waves could be generated by high frequency currents and the discovery of such radiation by Hertz that first convinced everyone that Maxwell's equations did contain the whole of electromagnetism. They form the starting point of the sequel to this text, *Electromagnetism*.

Appendix 1
Electric and magnetic quantities

Quantity	Symbol	Units	Dimensions	Equation
Electric current	I	A	A	S.I. unit
Electric charge	q	C	AT	[4.2]
Electric dipole moment	$\mathbf{p}$	$C\,m$	ALT	[2.26]
Electric field	$\mathbf{E}$	$V\,m^{-1}$	$A^{-1}MLT^{-3}$	[2.4]
Electric potential	ϕ	V	$A^{-1}ML^{2}T^{-3}$	[2.12]
Capacitance	C	F	$A^{2}M^{-1}L^{-2}T^{4}$	[2.19]
Electrostatic energy	U	J	$ML^{2}T^{-2}$	[2.36]
Polarisation	$\mathbf{P}$	$C\,m^{-2}$	$AL^{-2}T$	$\Sigma\mathbf{p}/\mathrm{vol}$
Electric susceptibility	χ_e	—	none	$\mathbf{P}/\epsilon_0\mathbf{E}$
Dielectric constant (relative permittivity)	ϵ_r	—	none	$(1 + \chi_e)$
Electric displacement	$\mathbf{D}$	$C\,m^{-2}$	$AL^{-2}T$	$\epsilon_0\mathbf{E}+\mathbf{P}$
Electric charge density	ρ	$C\,m^{-3}$	$AL^{-3}T$	q/vol
Surface charge density	σ	$C\,m^{-2}$	$AL^{-2}T$	q/area
Electric current density	$\mathbf{j}$	$A\,m^{-2}$	AL^{-2}	$q/\mathrm{area/s}$
Electrical conductivity	σ	$S\,m^{-1}$	$A^{-2}M^{-1}L^{-3}T^{3}$	$\mathbf{j}/\mathbf{E}$
Electrical resistance	R	Ω	$A^{-2}ML^{2}T^{3}$	[4.7]
Electromotive force	$\mathcal{E}$	V	$A^{-1}ML^{2}T^{-3}$	[5.1]
Magnetic field	$\mathbf{B}$	T	$A^{-1}MT^{-2}$	[4.8]
Magnetic dipole moment	$\mathbf{m}$	$A\,m^{2}$	AL^{2}	[4.12]
Magnetic flux	Φ	Wb	$A^{-1}ML^{2}T^{-2}$	[4.28]
Inductance, mutual	M	H	$A^{-2}MLT^{-2}$	[5.11]
Inductance, self	L	H	$A^{-2}MLT^{-2}$	[5.14]
Magnetisation	$\mathbf{M}$	$A\,m^{-1}$	AL^{-1}	$\Sigma\mathbf{m}/\mathrm{vol}$
Magnetising field	$\mathbf{H}$	$A\,m^{-1}$	AL^{-1}	$(\mathbf{B}/\mu_0)-\mathbf{M}$
Magnetic susceptibility	χ_m	—	none	$\mathbf{M}/\mathbf{H}$
Relative permeability	μ_r	—	none	$(1 + \chi_m)$
Surface current density	i	$A\,m^{-1}$	AL^{-1}	[6.3]
Magnetostatic energy	U	J	$ML^{2}T^{-2}$	[6.15]
Larmor frequency	ω_L	s^{-1}	T^{-1}	[6.20]
Magnetomotive force	$\mathscr{F}$	A	A	[6.29]
Magnetic reluctance	$\mathscr{R}$	$A\,Wb^{-1}$	$A^{2}M^{-1}L^{-2}T^{2}$	[6.29]

Appendix 2
Physical constants

Constant	Symbol	Value
Electric constant	$\epsilon_0 = 1/(\mu_0 c^2)$	$8.85 \times 10^{-12}\,\mathrm{F\,m^{-1}}$
Magnetic constant	μ_0	$4\pi \times 10^{-7}\,\mathrm{H\,m^{-1}}$
Speed of light	c	$3.00 \times 10^{8}\,\mathrm{m\,s^{-1}}$
Electronic charge	e	$1.60 \times 10^{-19}\,\mathrm{C}$
Rest mass of electron	m_e	$9.11 \times 10^{-31}\,\mathrm{kg}$
Rest mass of proton	m_p	$1.67 \times 10^{-27}\,\mathrm{kg}$
Planck constant	h	$6.63 \times 10^{-34}\,\mathrm{J\,s}$
	$\hbar = h/2\pi$	$1.05 \times 10^{-34}\,\mathrm{J\,s}$
Boltzmann constant	k	$1.38 \times 10^{-23}\,\mathrm{J\,K^{-1}}$
Avogadro number	N_A	$6.02 \times 10^{23}\,\mathrm{mol^{-1}}$
Gravitational constant	G	$6.67 \times 10^{-11}\,\mathrm{N\,m^2\,kg^{-2}}$
Bohr radius	$a_0 = \dfrac{4\pi\epsilon_0 \hbar^2}{m_\mathrm{e}^2}$	$5.29 \times 10^{-11}\,\mathrm{m}$
Bohr magneton	$\mu_\mathrm{B} = \dfrac{e\hbar}{2m_\mathrm{e}}$	$9.27 \times 10^{-24}\,\mathrm{J\,T^{-1}}$
Electron volt	eV	$1.60 \times 10^{-19}\,\mathrm{J}$
Molar volume at S.T.P.	V_m	$2.24 \times 10^{-2}\,\mathrm{m^3\,mol^{-1}}$
Acceleration due to gravity	g	$9.81\,\mathrm{m\,s^{-2}}$

Appendix 3
Vector operators

Scalar and vector fields may be operated on by the differential operators grad, div, curl and ∇^2. Expressions for the results of these operators in three coordinate systems are given below, with reference to the original equation where it is in the text.

Cartesian coordinates (x, y, z)

$$\text{grad } \Omega = \nabla\Omega = \frac{\partial\Omega}{\partial x}\mathbf{i} + \frac{\partial\Omega}{\partial y}\mathbf{j} + \frac{\partial\Omega}{\partial z}\mathbf{k} \qquad [2.16]$$

$$\text{div } \mathbf{F} = \nabla.\mathbf{F} = \frac{\partial F_x}{\partial x} + \frac{\partial F_y}{\partial y} + \frac{\partial F_z}{\partial z} \qquad [3.10]$$

$$\text{curl } \mathbf{F} = \nabla \times \mathbf{F} = \begin{vmatrix} \mathbf{i} & \mathbf{j} & \mathbf{k} \\ \dfrac{\partial}{\partial x} & \dfrac{\partial}{\partial y} & \dfrac{\partial}{\partial z} \\ F_x & F_y & F_z \end{vmatrix} \qquad [3.11]$$

$$\text{div (grad)} = \nabla^2 = \frac{\partial^2}{\partial x^2} + \frac{\partial^2}{\partial y^2} + \frac{\partial^2}{\partial z^2} \qquad [3.12]$$

Spherical polar coordinates (r, θ, ψ) see Fig. 2.5

$$\text{grad } \Omega = \frac{\partial\Omega}{\partial r}\hat{\mathbf{r}} + \frac{1}{r}\frac{\partial\Omega}{\partial\theta}\hat{\boldsymbol{\theta}} + \frac{1}{r\sin\theta}\frac{\partial\Omega}{\partial\psi}\hat{\boldsymbol{\psi}} \qquad [3.17]$$

$$\text{div } \mathbf{F} = \frac{1}{r^2}\frac{\partial}{\partial r}(r^2 F_r) + \frac{1}{r\sin\theta}\frac{\partial}{\partial\theta}(\sin\theta F_\theta) + \frac{1}{r\sin\theta}\frac{\partial F_\psi}{\partial\psi}$$

$$\text{curl } \mathbf{F} = \frac{1}{r^2 \sin\theta} \begin{vmatrix} \hat{\mathbf{r}} & r\hat{\boldsymbol{\theta}} & r\sin\theta\hat{\boldsymbol{\psi}} \\ \dfrac{\partial}{\partial r} & \dfrac{\partial}{\partial \theta} & \dfrac{\partial}{\partial \psi} \\ F_r & rF_\theta & r\sin\theta F_\psi \end{vmatrix}$$

$$\nabla^2 = \frac{1}{r^2}\frac{\partial}{\partial r}\left(r^2\frac{\partial}{\partial r}\right) + \frac{1}{r^2\sin\theta}\frac{\partial}{\partial \theta}\left(\sin\theta\frac{\partial}{\partial \theta}\right) + \frac{1}{r^2\sin^2\theta}\frac{\partial^2}{\partial \psi^2}$$

$$[3.16]$$

Cylindrical polar coordinates (r, θ, z) see Fig. 3.2

$$\text{grad } \Omega = \frac{\partial \Omega}{\partial r}\hat{\mathbf{r}} + \frac{\partial \Omega}{r\partial \theta}\hat{\boldsymbol{\theta}} + \frac{\partial \Omega}{\partial z}\hat{\mathbf{z}}$$

$$\text{div } \mathbf{F} = \frac{1}{r}\frac{\partial}{\partial r}(rF_r) + \frac{\partial F_\theta}{r\partial \theta} + \frac{\partial F_z}{\partial z}$$

$$\text{curl } \mathbf{F} = \frac{1}{r} \begin{vmatrix} \hat{\mathbf{r}} & r\hat{\boldsymbol{\theta}} & \hat{\mathbf{z}} \\ \dfrac{\partial}{\partial r} & \dfrac{\partial}{\partial \theta} & \dfrac{\partial}{\partial z} \\ F_r & rF_\theta & F_z \end{vmatrix}$$

$$\nabla^2 = \frac{1}{r}\frac{\partial}{\partial r}\left(r\frac{\partial}{\partial r}\right) + \frac{1}{r^2}\frac{\partial^2}{\partial \theta^2} + \frac{\partial^2}{\partial z^2}$$

$$[3.18]$$

Appendix 4
Exercises

(L) indicates University of London question.

Chapter 2

1   Compare the magnitudes of the electrostatic and gravitational forces between two alphas particles (He^{2+}).

2   A charge of 111 pC is uniformly distributed throughout the volume of an isolated sphere of diameter 40 cm. Calculate the electric field at the following distances from the centre of the sphere: (a) zero; (b) 10 cm; (c) 20 cm; (d) 50 cm.   (L)

3   How much work is done on an electron when it is moved from (3, 2, −1) to (2, 1, −4) in an electric field given by $E = (3i - 4j + 2k) \, V \, m^{-1}$? (Distance in metres)   (L)

4   A charge of $3 \, \mu C$ is uniformly distributed along a thin rod of length 40 cm. Find the electric field at a point 20 cm from the rod on its perpendicular bisector.

5   Show from first principles that the dimensions of capacitance are $A^2 M^{-1} L^{-2} T^4$ on the M.K.S.A. (S.I.) system and find the dimensions of the electric constant, ϵ_0.

6   An electron moves from rest through a displacement $(10^{-3}i + 10^{-3}j + 10^{-3}k)$ metres within an electric field $(10^5 i + 10^5 j + 10^5 k) \, V \, m^{-1}$. Find: (a) the kinetic energy gained by the electron; (b) its final velocity.

7   Prove that the capacitance of an isolated sphere of radius a is $4\pi\epsilon_0 a$.

8   Eight identical spherical drops of mercury are each charged to

10 V above earth (ground) potential and then allowed to coalesce into a single spherical drop. What is the potential of the large drop? How has the electrostatic energy of the system changed?

(L)

9   A spherical electrode is required to carry a charge of 33 nC. Estimate its minimum radius if the breakdown field strength of the surrounding air is $3 \times 10^6 \,V\,m^{-1}$.

10   Two isolated metal spheres of radii 40 and 90 mm are charged to 0.9 and 2.0 kV respectively. They are then connected by a fine wire. Explain what happens to: (a) the electric charges; (b) the electric potentials; (c) the electrical energy stored in the system. Hence find (d) the stored energy lost as a result of the connection.

11   A 12 pF parallel-plate air capacitor is charged by connecting it to a 100 V battery. How much work must be done to double the separation of the plates of the capacitor: (a) with the battery connected; (b) with it disconnected and the capacitor fully charged? Explain why the answers differ.

12   A large parallel plate capacitor is completely filled by a 2 mm thick slab of a dielectric ($\epsilon_r = 6$) and a 1 mm thick slab of another dielectric ($\epsilon_r = 2$). The plates are connected to a 1 kV battery, the plate next to the thick layer being positive and the other earthed (grounded). Calculate: (a) the surface charge density on the plates; and (b) the potential at the dielectric interface.

(L)

13   A long coaxial cable consists of an inner wire radius a inside a metal tube of inside radius b, the space in between being completely filled with a dielectric of relative permittivity ϵ_r. Show that its capacitance is $(2\pi\epsilon_r\epsilon_0)/(lnb/a)$ F m^{-1}. (Hint: Use Gauss's law for the electric displacement flux.)

14   A parallel plate capacitor consists of rectangular plates of length a and width b spaced d apart connected to a battery of voltage V. A rectangular slab of dielectric of relative permittivity ϵ_r that would just fill the space between the capacitor plates is inserted part way between them, so that it resembles a partly opened matchbox. Show that the force pulling it into the plates is $(\epsilon_r - 1)(\epsilon_0 bV^2)/(2d)$ and explain why it is independent of a.

Chapter 3

1 An electric dipole of moment $\mathbf{p} = q\mathbf{a}$ is placed with its centre at the origin and its axis along $\theta = 0$, where (r, θ, ψ) are spherical polar coordinates. Show that the potential $\phi(r, \theta, \psi)$, for $r \gg a$, is independent of ψ and given by $(\mathbf{p} \cdot \mathbf{r})/(4\pi\epsilon_0 r^3)$. Hence show that the electric field at a point (r, θ) has amplitude

$$\frac{p}{4\pi\epsilon_0 r^3} (1 + 3\cos^2\theta)^{\frac{1}{2}} \qquad (L)$$

2 Using the expressions in exercise 1, plot the equipotentials and field lines for a dipole and compare them with those for a point charge.

3 A pair of electric dipoles are placed end-on in a straight line so that their negative charges coincide and they form a linear quadrupole of length $2a$ with charges $+q$ at each end and $-2q$ in the centre. Given that the electric field on the axis of a dipole at a distance $r \gg a$ is $(2qa)/(4\pi\epsilon_0 r^3)$, find the electric field on the axis of the quadrupole at a distance $r(r \gg a)$ from its centre.

4 Show that a dipole of moment $\mathbf{p}$ placed in a uniform electric field $\mathbf{E}$ acquires a potential energy $-\mathbf{p} \cdot \mathbf{E}$ and that a couple $\mathbf{p} \times \mathbf{E}$ acts to align it with the field.

5 A conducting sphere of radius R is placed in a uniform electric field $\mathbf{E}_0$. Show that the potential at a point outside the sphere and at (r, θ) from its centre is

$$-E_0 r \cos\theta \ \{1 - (R^3)/(r^3)\}$$

and hence find the components E_r and E_θ of the electric field at that point.

6 An isotropic dielectric sphere of radius R and dielectric constant ϵ_1, is placed in a medium of dielectric constant ϵ_2 containing a uniform electric field $\mathbf{E}_0$. Show that the potentials at points (r, θ) from the centre of the sphere are

(a) $-3\epsilon_2 E_0 r \cos\theta/(\epsilon_1 + 2\epsilon_2)$

inside the sphere and

(b) $-E_0 r \cos\theta \left\{1 - \left(\dfrac{\epsilon_1 - \epsilon_2}{\epsilon_1 + 2\epsilon_2}\right)\dfrac{R^3}{r^3}\right\}$

outside it. Hence draw the lines of electric displacement **D** inside and outside the sphere when $\epsilon_1 < \epsilon_2$ and $\epsilon_1 > \epsilon_2$. (Hint: Assume that the potentials are of the same form as that for the conducting sphere and apply the boundary conditions to obtain the coefficients in each case.)

7 A long cylindrical conductor of radius R is earthed and placed in a uniform electric field $\mathbf{E_0}$ with its axis normal to $\mathbf{E_0}$. Show that the potential at a point (r, θ, z) is

$$\phi = E_0 r \cos\theta \, \{1 - (a^2)/(r^2)\}$$

(Hint: Show that this solution satisfies Laplace's equation and the boundary conditions.)

8 Show that a positive charge placed at $(4, 2)$ between conducting planes $y = 0$ and $x = y$ produces the same electric field between the planes as a system of four positive and four negative charges and find the positions of these charges. Will this method work for any angle between the planes?

9 Use the method of images to show that an uncharged, insulated conducting sphere of radius R is attracted to a positive charge q_1 at a distance r from its centre by the force:

$$\frac{q_1{}^2}{4\pi\epsilon_o} \left[\frac{R}{r^3} - \frac{R}{r\{r - (R^2)/(r)\}^2} \right]$$

(Hint: Find the image charge for an earthed (grounded) sphere first.)

10 A dipole of moment **p** is placed at a distance r from the centre of an earthed conducting sphere of radius $R < r$. The axis of the dipole is in the direction from the centre of the sphere to the centre of the dipole. Prove that the image system for the dipole is a point charge pR/r^2 plus a dipole of strength pR^3/r^3 and find their positions.

Chapter 4

1 The current density in a long conductor of circular cross-section and radius R varies with radius as $j = j_0 r^2$. Calculate the current flowing in the conductor.

2 An earthing (grounding) plate is formed from a hemispherical

spinning of copper sheet placed in the earth with its rim at the earth's surface. Calculate its earthing resistance, given that its diameter is 0.5 m and the conductivity of the earth is 0.01 S m^{-1}.

3   Calculate the magnitude and direction of the magnetic field at the centre of a short solenoid of radius 3 cm and length 8 cm carrying a current of 10 A and having 8 turns per cm.   (L)

4   Show that the magnetic field at the ends and on the axis of a long solenoid is half that at its centre.

5   A Helmholtz pair consists of two identical circular coils of radius a carrying the same current I in the same direction mounted coaxially an optimum distance b apart to give the maximum volume of uniform magnetic field between them. Show that this is achieved when $b = a$ and find the uniform field. (Hint: If the axis of the coils is the x-axis, show that $\partial B/\partial x$ and $\partial^2 B/\partial x^2$ are zero for B on the axis.)

6   An electron is moving at 2×10^6 m s^{-1} round a circular orbit of radius 5×10^{-11} m. What is the magnetic field at the centre of the orbit?

7   Calculate the force per unit length on each of a pair of parallel wires 5 cm apart carrying the same current of 500 A. What happens when one of the currents is reversed?   (L)

8   Calculate the magnetic field at the centre of a square wire loop of sides 10 cm in length carrying a current of 10 A. (Hint: Consider each side separately.)

9   A steady current I flows in one direction in the solid inner conductor, radius a, of a coaxial cable and in the opposite direction in the outer conductor, of inner radius b and outer radius c. Find the magnetic field at a distance r from the axis in each of the following regions: (a) $r \leqslant a$; (b) $a \leqslant r \leqslant b$; (c) $b \leqslant r \leqslant c$; (d) $r \geqslant c$.

10 Find the magnetic dipole moment of an electron moving in an orbit with a Bohr radius a_0.

Chapter 5

1   A current loop of area S in the xy plane is placed in a uniform magnetic field $B_z = B_0 \sin \omega t$. Find the e.m.f. induced in the coil: (a) when it is fixed; (b) when it rotates at an angular frequency ω.

2   An aircraft with a wingspan of 50 m flies horizontally at 300 m s^{-1} through a vertical magnetic field of 20μT. What is the potential difference between the wing tips?

3   Estimate the kinetic energy in MeV of the electrons in a betatron when they are travelling along an orbit of radius 0.25 m in a magnetic field of 0.5 T. (Hint: High-speed electrons travel at nearly the speed of light.)

4   A thin metal disc of 5 cm radius is mounted on an axle of 1 cm radius and rotated at 2,400 revolutions per minute in a uniform magnetic field of 0.4 T. Brushes, connected in parallel, make contact with many points on the rim of the disc, and another set of brushes make similar contacts with the axle. The resistance measured between the sets of brushes due to the disc is $100 \mu\Omega$. Calculate the magnitude and direction of the current flowing in the disc. *(L)*

5   A solenoid of 1000 turns is 2 cm in diameter and 10 cm long. Estimate the energy stored in it when it is carrying 100 A. *(L)*

6   Calculate the mutual inductance between a very long solenoid with 200 turns per metre and a circular coil consisting of 50 turns of mean area 20 cm^2 placed coaxially inside the solenoid. *(L)*

7   A large solenoid of radius 5 cm is wound uniformly with 1000 turns per metre and has a secondary winding of 500 turns closely wound over its centre portion. If a sinusoidal current of 2 A r.m.s. and frequency 50 Hz is passed through the solenoid, what is the e.m.f. induced in the secondary?

8   An ignition coil consisting of 16 000 turns wound closely on a solenoid of 400 turns and length 10 cm has a radius of 3 cm. If the primary current of 3 A is broken 10 000 times each second by the car's motion, what is the voltage produced across the spark plugs?

9   A long transmission line consists of two thin, parallel metal strips each 1 cm wide facing each other across a 5 cm gap. What is the inductance per metre of the line? (Hint: Consider the strips to be segments of an infinite circular, coaxial line.)

Chapter 6

1   A long paramagnetic circular rod of diameter 6 mm is suspended vertically from a balance so that one end is between the poles of an electromagnet providing a horizontal magnetic field of 1.5 T and the other end is in a negligible field. If the apparent increase in mass of the rod is 5 g, what is the magnetic susceptibility of the material? (Hint: Use the principle of virtual work to relate force to energy.)

2   Calculate the total magnetic energy in the earth's external field by assuming it is due to a dipole at the centre of the earth producing a magnetic field of 1 gauss at the equator. (Assume the radius of the earth is 6400 km.)

3   State whether the following statements are true or false in the MKSA system. (a) $\mathbf{B}$ and $\mathbf{H}$ are the same physical quantity but are measured in different units. (b) In free space $\mathbf{B} = \mu_0 \mathbf{H}$ means that $\mathbf{B}$ measures the response of a vacuum to the applied field $\mathbf{H}$. (c) In matter $\mathbf{H}$ is the volume average of the microscopic value of $\mathbf{B}$, multiplied by a factor independent of the material. (d) In matter if $\mathbf{H}$, $\mathbf{B}$ and $\mathbf{M}$ are smoothed to remove irregularities on an atomic scale, then $\mathbf{B}$ is the sum of $\mathbf{H}$ and $\mathbf{M}$, multiplied by a factor independent of the material. (e) The sources of $\mathbf{H}$ are magnetic poles and of $\mathbf{B}$ are electric currents.

4   An intense magnetic field pulse is generated by discharging rapidly a bank of 1000 5 μF capacitors, wired in parallel, through a short, strong coil of inductance 10 mH and volume 10 cm^3. If the capacitors are charged to 1.5 kV before discharge, calculate: (a) the maximum magnetic field produced; (b) the maximum current; (c) the time to reach the maximum field. (Hint: Assume a sinusoidal discharge.)

5   An electromagnet consists of a soft iron ring of mean radius 8 cm with an air gap of 3 mm. It is wound with 100 turns carrying a current of 3 A. Given that the B–H curve for soft iron has the following characteristics, determine the magnetic field in the gap:

B(T)	0.2	0.4	0.6	0.8	1.0
H(A m^{-1})	100	170	220	310	500

Appendix 5
Answers to exercises

Chapter 2

1   3.10×10^{35}.
2   (a) 0   (b) $12.5\ \mathrm{V\,m^{-1}}$ (c) $25\ \mathrm{V\,m^{-1}}$ (d) $4\ \mathrm{V\,m^{-1}}$.
3    $8 \times 10^{-19}\ \mathrm{J}$.
4    $4.77 \times 10^{5}\ \mathrm{V\,m^{-1}}$.
5    $\mathrm{A^{2}\,M^{-1}\,L^{-3}\,T^{4}}$.
6   (a) $4.80 \times 10^{-17}\ \mathrm{J}$ (b) $1.03 \times 10^{7}\ \mathrm{m\,s^{-1}}$.
8    $40\ \mathrm{V}$; increased fourfold.
9    $10\ \mathrm{mm}$.
10   (a) Total charge of 24 nC is conserved. (b) Potentials equalised to 1.66 kV by charge flow. (c) Some energy lost to Joulean heat in wire and flash of light (spark). (d) $1.9\ \mu\mathrm{J}$.
11   (a) $3 \times 10^{-8}\ \mathrm{J}$ (b) $6 \times 10^{-8}\ \mathrm{J}$. In (a) $6 \times 10^{-8}\ \mathrm{J}$ work is done charging the battery, but work done on capacitor is $-3 \times 10^{-8}\ \mathrm{J}$.
12   (a) $10.8\ \mu\mathrm{C\ m^{-2}}$ (b) $600\ \mathrm{V}$.
14   Force acts only where the electric field is non-uniform, at the edge of the plates over the dielectric.

Chapter 3

1    $\phi = (p \cos\theta)/(4\pi\epsilon_{0} r^{2})$.
3    $(3qa^{2})/(2\pi\epsilon_{0} r^{4})$.
5    $E_{r} = E_{0}\cos\theta\,\{1 + 2\,(R^{3}/r^{3})\};\ E_{\theta} = -E_{0}\sin\theta\,\{1 - (R^{3}/r^{3})\}$.
6   Lines of **D** are continuous and uniform within the sphere, but forced out when $\epsilon_{1} < \epsilon_{2}$ and forced in when $\epsilon_{1} > \epsilon_{2}$.

8   Positive at $(-2, 4)$, $(-4, -2)$, $(2, -4)$, $(4, 2)$; negative at $(2, 4)$, $(-4, 2)$, $(-2, 4)$, $(4, -2)$. No, angle must be submultiple of 2π.

10 Both at a point inverse to the centre of the dipole in the sphere.

Chapter 4

1   $\pi j_0 R^4 / 2$.

2   $63.7\,\Omega$.

3   $8.04 \times 10^{-3}\,\text{T}$.

5   $8\mu_0 I / (5\sqrt{5}\,a)$.

6   $12.8\,\text{T}$.

7   $1.00\,\text{Nm}^{-1}$. Same direction, attractive; opposite direction, repulsive.

8   $1.13 \times 10^{-4}\,\text{T}$.

9   (a) $\mu_0 Ir / (2\pi a^2)$ (b) $\mu_0 I / (2\pi r)$ (c) $\dfrac{\mu_0 I}{2\pi r}\left(\dfrac{c^2 - r^2}{c^2 - b^2}\right)$ (d) 0.

10 1 Bohr magneton $= 9.27 \times 10^{-24}\,\text{J T}^{-1}$.

Chapter 5

1   (a) $B_0 S\omega \cos \omega t$ (b) $B_0 S\omega \cos 2\omega t$.

2   $0.3\,\text{V}$.

3   $37.5\,\text{MeV}$.

4   $1.21\,\text{kA}$. For motion clockwise about **B**, current flows from centre to rim.

5   $1.97\,\text{kJ}$.

6   $25.1\,\mu\text{H}$.

7   $3.14\,\text{V r.m.s.}$

8   $6.82\,\text{kV}$.

9   $6.28\,\mu\text{H}$.

Chapter 6

1 1.96×10^{-3}.

2 2.83×10^{19} J.

3 (a) False, since they have different dimensions. (b) False; this just defines the units of **H**. (c) False; $H = (\vec{B}_a/\mu_0) - N\bar{m}$ always has finite $\bar{m}$, although it can be very small. (d) True; $\mathbf{B} = \mu_0(\mathbf{H} + \mathbf{M})$. (e) False; sources of **H** are conduction currents and of **B** are conduction and magnetisation currents.

4 (a) 37.6 T (b) 1.12 kA (c) 11.1 ms.

5 0.71 T.

Index

solenoids: Bitter, 98; magnetic field, 65, 118; superconducting, 98

speed of light c, 5, 111

spherical coordinates, 9, 34

Stokes's theorem, 33, 72

superconductors, 87, 98

superposition, principle of, 5

surface charge density σ, 110; free σ_f, 24; of polarised dielectric σ_p, 24

surface current density: i, 110; of magnetised matter i_m, 81

susceptibility: electric χ_e, 26, 110; magnetic χ_m, 84, 90, 92, 110

tesla, unit of magnetic field, 54, 65

test charge, 15

Thomson, J.J., vii

torque: on electric dipole, 57, 116; on magnetic dipole, 57, 91

transmission line, 119

uniqueness theorem, 37

units, viii, 110

vector operators, 112ff

velocity of light c, 5, 111

volt, unit of electric potential, 17

watt, unit of electric power, 71

weber, unit of magnetic flux, 65

Weiss electromagnet, 100

work: electrical, 14, 21, 79; virtual, 30, 102

Series Editor:
Professor R. J. Blin-Stoyle, FRS
Professor of Theoretical Physics, University of Sussex

The aim of the *Student Physics Series* is to cover the material
required for a first degree course in physics in a series of concise,
clear and readable texts. Each volume will cover one of the usual
sections of the physics degree course and will concentrate on
covering the essential features of the subject. The texts will thus
provide a core course in physics that all students should be
expected to acquire, and to which more advanced work can be
related according to ability. By concentrating on the essentials,
the texts should also allow a valuable perspective and
accessibility not normally attainable through the more usual
textbooks.

QUANTUM MECHANICS

Quantum mechanics is the key to modern physics, yet it is notoriously hard to learn. This book is designed to overcome that obstacle. Clear and concise, it provides an easily readable introduction intended for science undergraduates with no previous knowledge of the quantum theory, and takes them up to final-year level.

The emphasis is on clarity, achieved by focusing on the essential features of the subject and excluding much of the technical padding which characterizes more developed discussions in longer books. The style is informal, and the author uses his wide experience as a writer and broadcaster on 'popular science' to explain the many difficult abstract points of the subject in easily comprehensible language and imagery.

P. C. W. Davies

Professor Paul Davies is Professor of Theoretical Physics at the University of Newcastle upon Tyne.

ISBN 0-7100-9962-2
160 pp., 198mm x 129mm, diagrams

RELATIVITY PHYSICS

Relativity Physics covers all the material required for a first course in relativity. Beginning with an examination of the paradoxes that arose in applying the principle of relativity to the two great pillars of nineteenth-century physics—classical mechanics and electromagnetism—Dr Turner shows how Einstein resolved these problems in a spectacular and brilliantly intuitive way. The implications of Einstein's postulates are then discussed and the book concludes with a discussion of the charged particle in the electromagnetic field.

The text incorporates details of the most recent experiments and includes applications to high-energy physics, astronomy, and solid state physics. Exercises with answers are included for the student.

R. E. Turner

Dr Roy Turner is Reader in Theoretical Physics at the University of Sussex.

ISBN 0-7102-0001-3
16 0 pp., 198 mm × 129 mm, diagrams

CLASSICAL MECHANICS

A course in classical mechanics is an essential requirement of any first degree course in physics. In this volume Dr Brian Cowan provides a clear, concise and self-contained introduction to the subject and covers all the material needed by a student taking such a course. The author treats the material from a modern viewpoint, culminating in a final chapter showing how the Lagrangian and Hamiltonian formulations lend themselves particularly well to the more 'modern' areas of physics such as quantum mechanics. Worked examples are included in the text and there are exercises, with answers, for the student.

B. P. Cowan

Dr Brian Cowan is in the Department of Physics, Bedford College, University of London

ISBN 0-7102-0280-6
128 pp., 198 mm x 129 mm, diagrams